Rooted and Refreshed

TIFFANY FOX

Rooted & Refreshed: A 90-Day Devotional for Teachers

Published by MrsTFox Resources.

To protect the privacy of individuals mentioned in this book, most names and identifying details have been changed. Where a real name was retained, permission was granted.

All Hebrew and Greek translations are taken from the Blue Letter Bible.

ISBN: 979-8-9933467-0-0

Printed in the United States of America

This devotional is the perfect addition to any teacher's desk! Mrs. Fox has mastered building effective student relationships and curriculum, but now she has knocked it out of the ball park, creating a reflective and centering space for teachers to recharge and refocus on their practice. The devotional is a personal space that allows quiet affirmations that will energize teaching practices. Excellent!!

—Jennifer Douglas, Educator

This book gets right to the heart of the matter; whether you're a teacher or not. I work with students at church, and the "Graceful Authority" devotion touched me and reminded me that life's not about me but that I am called to behave like Jesus. Thank you, Tiffany Fox, for using God's truths and your humor to root and refresh all who read this book!

—Cheri Thompson

I could not put this book down. I loved the book, and I know all readers will too. Though it was written for teachers, Tiffany's words and devotions ring true for every walk of life.

—Beverly Formato

The devotional book is fantastic. As a believer, I very much needed to read it and will continue to. It is desperately needed by teachers all around the country. We are worn out for various reasons! This devotional gave me much to relate to and reflect on as I look at my own instructional practice, especially from a Christian perspective.

—Jay Linsberger, Educator

Rooted and Refreshed has been a balm to me. It speaks into all I experience as a teacher and gently guides me to Christ. There is so much to fill my day, but it is refreshing to pause and reflect on God's purpose for each season. I am so thankful for Tiffany's obedience to the Lord to write this—her mentorship has been invaluable to me!

—Alicia Zyskowski, Educator

It doesn't matter what age you teach—this book is for all teachers. Having had the privilege of being Tiffany's cooperating teacher when she was a student teacher, I learned as much from her as she did from her experience. Now that I am a friend of Tiffany Fox, I can honestly attest to her dedication, faith, and ability to touch your heart with her devotions.

—Patte Elder, Educator

As I am reading, I'm crying, smiling, relating, laughing, picking up my Bible, and thinking who all to share this powerful devotional with. It's not just for teachers by profession—in a sense, we all are teachers. What a wonderful, inspiring work Tiffany has written.

—Ava Cooley

Rooted and Refreshed has taken me on a beautiful trip down memory lane. From the introduction to the daily reflections, I found myself revisiting both past and present moments in my classroom and personal life. This experience mirrors the journey God takes us on each day—teaching us to learn from the past and to lean on Him for guidance when life throws us a curveball. Tiffany, God is clearly using you to share His Word through your own journey. *Rooted and Refreshed* offers the perfect opportunity to step away from the busyness of life, reconnect with God's Word, and reflect on how it guides your daily walk

—John Hutchinson, Educator

The stories inside this devotional are so moving and powerful. Tiffany has a real gift for writing, and this devotional gives a new perspective on how to approach teaching with faith at the center—every chapter is a little pep talk about how we can see our school and classrooms in a new light, how we can bring kindness and encouragement to others. My favorite takeaway is that all the students in your classroom are God's children, entrusted to us for this chapter in their lives, and each one is meant to be there for a reason. This is a powerful book that will encourage teachers at every step in their journey. Thank you for sharing it with us!

—Marcia Beckett, Educator

Even if you are not spiritual or religious, there is something valuable in each of the devotions. It is nice to read about common teacher experiences and think about how to reframe responses to similar situations.

—Kelly Ryan, Educator

Tiffany is as masterful with her words as she is with her art. She truly understands what it means to be a teacher. Her devotions are encouraging and empowering. Her book touches this teacher's heart and soul.

—Rachel Mills, Educator

Even from the first few pages of Rooted and Refreshed I was thinking to myself, "She gets it." This is a powerful book that will encourage teachers at every step in their journey. Thank you, Tiffany Fox, for sharing it with us!

—Corrie Soderlund, Educator

A beautiful read.

—Travis Fitzwater

This book is dedicated to my dear friend Cheri Thompson—
You've been there since the very first nudge God placed on my heart, listening, cheering, and faithfully reminding me to finish the race. Thank you for speaking truth when I needed it. Your encouragement helped these pages find their way into the world.

How to Begin Each Day Rooted and Refreshed

This devotional was created for the busiest of teachers—the ones juggling lesson plans, emails, lunch duty, and the constant swirl of classroom energy. *Rooted and Refreshed* isn't meant to be another task on your to-do list. It's meant to refill you—one quiet, intentional moment at a time.

Each day includes a short Scripture, a "Rooted" heartfelt reflection, and a "Refreshed" prompt to help you refocus your heart, even on days that feel like a blur. You don't need a perfect routine to benefit from this book—just a willing heart and a few minutes to breathe.

Here's how to make the most of it:

- **Read the daily entry** whenever you can—during your morning coffee, lunch break, or right before bed. There's no schedule to keep or pressure to catch up.
- **Reflect on the "Refreshed" section.** These simple prompts are designed to help you stay rooted in your purpose and connected to God, even in the busiest seasons.
- **Respond in the space provided.** Use the box at the end of each entry to jot a few thoughts, scribble a prayer, or doodle what's on your heart. There's no wrong way to use it—just make it yours.

Let this book be your quiet companion—a place to pause, realign, and remember that even in the chaos, your calling is sacred and your soul matters.

Introduction

"Mrs. Fox, when do you think you'll retire?"

"Never. I'll die right here in this room, teaching your grandchildren."

In 2020 if you had asked me "Where do you see yourself in five years?" it certainly wouldn't have been here writing a devotional. Not a chance, my friend.

But here you are, reading a devotional written by me. Isn't it just like God to have the last word? In this particular case, he has all 65,000 of them.

Between the years 2009 and 2022, Lake Norman High School in Mooresville, North Carolina, was my sanctuary, the place where I taught art to high schoolers. A beautiful school with a wonderful leadership team, a robust visual-arts budget, and supportive, encouraging coworkers. It was the only teaching job I ever had, and it was glorious.

I'm typing with my eyes closed, smiling as I reflect on a typical day at the high school. It's 7:00 a.m. I'm moving gingerly, loaded down with teacher stuff as I make my way down Hollywood Hall (the art hallway) toward my room. Glaring fluorescent lights bounce off the freshly mopped tile floors. I can still hear the two-clunk cadence of the metal handle as I press down and push on the door. Students are already inside. Light chatter and laughter remind me what a blessing teaching truly is.

A series of family-centered circumstances—explained in a couple of the devotions to follow—brought me out of my dream job and moved me to another state.

When you meet someone new, they usually ask, "So what do you do?"

"I teach high school." Cue the look of outright disgust. I might as well have said I gutted livestock. If you're an elementary school teacher, people smile and coo, but a high school teacher? Not so much.

My response was (and still is) that teaching is honestly the most wonderful vocation on the planet. Yes, the entire planet. And no, I haven't done all the jobs on the planet.

High school students are on the twenty-yard line, making their way to the end zone we call adulthood. Once they cross the threshold, it's game over—welcome to real life. Whether it's college or the military, the work force or parenthood, it's go-time.

As educators we are perfectly positioned to lay the foundation of skill sets, confidence, and courage. As you walk with me through this devotional, you'll see countless situations where God equipped me to meet students exactly where they were with exact provision—the same as he does for you. Sometimes I recognized it; other times I had no idea.

I viewed my classroom as a rest stop on the side of a bustling highway. Every eighteen weeks, another group of weary travelers stopped by, leaving their baggage outside along the road. During our time together, the mission was to realize our predetermined excellence. This group was divinely unique, and we would never be together with the same members ever again.

Late in 2022 I heard God calling me to write a devotional for teachers. My response for the better part of 2023 was simple. *No thanks. I'll pass.* Of all the talents I may possess, writing is not on the list. God's still, small voice never got louder, but it became increasingly more frequent. By the end of 2023, and after many failed attempts at ignoring the call, I considered the task.

The message went something like this: *Tiffany, teachers are hurting and under attack from all sides. They need to hear the good news that I am with them. I am the original resource, no matter the trial. I am their strength and their salvation. I am for them, not against them, and every one of my children is placed in their care for a purpose.*

During the consideration, the fear of the call increased. After a while I heard this: *Look how I carried you, provided for you, and handed you the best job ever. I showed up to school every day as more than one thousand of my beautiful children passed through your classroom on their way to adulthood. Trust me to give you the wisdom and the words.*

I wish I could tell you I had all the answers. That after reading this devotional you will never have another difficult day in education. Until 2022 I thought I'd die at my desk.

Teaching is a matchless experience. Whether we teach for one year or thirty, we have shaped another person's life as they traveled toward the end zone of adulthood. Are they in better shape now than before they entered our classroom?

I finally stopped wishing I was in room 357 and got busy listening to God. As it turns out, my time inside those four walls was preparation for this book.

The next time you open your classroom door and the laughter reaches your ears, consider your blessings.

You truly do have the best job ever.

1
Roadway in the Wilderness

Do not call to mind the former things,
Or consider things of the past.
Behold, I am going to do something new,
Now it will spring up;
Will you not be aware of it?
I will even make a roadway in the wilderness,
Rivers in the desert.

Isaiah 43:18–19

Thirteen.

The number of years I was blessed to be a high school teacher.

I never thought I would do anything but teach high school as long as I lived. An administrator once left this comment on my evaluation: "Ms. Fox is a born educator. Teaching is in her bones."

When I landed my first and only job teaching high school art, I knew I had finally found my calling. Unbeknown to me, it was preparation for a future calling.

Our only child had settled two hours away. When she got married the year before, I told my husband we would not miss out on knowing her children. In 2022 we relocated, leaving my original calling behind. It's now an eight-minute drive to enjoy every possible moment with her family. When our granddaughter was born, a lady in the waiting room said to me, "Being a grandparent is the only thing in life that isn't overrated." I now know how true this is.

In the early days after our move, I leaned heavily on verse 19. Being close to family is wonderful and running my own business is a blessing, but I missed the classroom and the students desperately.

This was a new chapter, and at times it felt like a wilderness. I delved full-time into curriculum design, developing lessons for secondary art educators. This opportunity to help teachers was both timely and fulfilling. I heard from teacher clients how their sanity was still intact from the time saved, as they no longer had to reinvent the wheel.

My drug of choice is helping people succeed. No matter who it is, be it students or coworkers or fellow educators. My mission is to come alongside people and leave them better than before they met me. God knows the desires of our hearts. What happened in the coming months revealed to me just how well he knows mine.

I felt God calling me to encourage my fellow educators. Over the past thirteen years, more than one person had mentioned that I should write a book. Talk about terrifying. Almost immediately I resisted the notion, with both heels in the dirt.

Make no mistake, I was both uncomfortable and irritated, but once I stopped resisting, the chance to help educators filled my soul with joy. Of course! I'll write a classroom-management guide! **No**, he said, **that's not it**. That's when things got even more intimidating. He whispered about writing a devotional.

"I'm no writer, and I'm certainly no theologian. What do I have to offer that could help anyone?"

In the early days after leaving teaching, my memory was constantly rewinding to my time in the classroom. I couldn't walk past a teenager without getting teary eyed.

You know how you keep replaying all those wonderful classroom memories? Start there.

We all share similar classroom experiences. We hear the same slang, deal with the same never-ending drama, struggle to motivate (and sometimes locate) our students. As you turn the pages of this book and we walk through my classroom for a few moments, we can be encouraged together, knowing we both love helping young people succeed.

When we recognize and focus on God's presence, we see him at work in our classrooms. I realized early on that the educational landscape is constantly shifting. Every year brings a fresh onslaught of change. New procedures, new expectations, and new data measurements—all of it making us physically ill as we consider the mountain of work looming in our classrooms.

What if we saw change through God's eyes, looking for the good he has in store? He says here in this passage that he is making a "roadway in the wilderness." A roadway is a strip of land over which a road passes. God is making room in our lives for us to pave a new road. This roadway will enable us to travel safely when we venture into uncharted territory.

Maybe you're on a road into a new classroom, a different school, or a district with an easier commute. You could be examining the potential of retirement or a career shift altogether. Whatever it is, God wants to accompany us in every scary place. He is our source of water in dry climates and our source of navigation in new spaces.

Rooted

In every changing season, look expectantly for the roadways. When all we see is wilderness, God is making a way.

Refreshed

Reflect on a time when you watched God make a roadway in a changing wilderness season.

2
Graceful Authority

In all things show yourself to be an example of good deeds, with purity in doctrine, dignified, sound in speech which is beyond reproach, so that the opponent will be put to shame, having nothing bad to say about us.

Titus 2:7–8

Seeking the approval of teenagers is futile. You may as well chase a butterfly bare-handed and blindfolded.

"But I want them to like me."

Here's the problem. Who they like or don't like changes with the wind. To make matters worse, this fickle admiration swings on the hinges of adolescent hormones. Anyone with me? I see you nodding.

A wise administrator once told me, "We want to be friendly with students, not friends with students." I know, I know. This can be tough, especially in our upper-level classes. A lot of personal discussions take place here. While the students need to talk about their ideas, the lines of authority that are clearly drawn avoid that slippery slope of "She's cool—she won't do anything."

In my first year teaching, I had what I thought was a firm stance with my advanced-level class, a small group of overachievers. We were working toward portfolio submission, and with the daily free exchange of ideas, the atmosphere had become casual. If you've taught advanced kids, you've probably been here. That line in the sand can easily be swept away.

One afternoon I sat at my desk, asking students one by one to bring me their sketchbooks for grading. A young man named Jordan sat three seats away from my desk, chatting with his neighbor. A girl named Sidney worked quietly in the seat next to me.

"Jordan, please bring me your sketchbook." No response. Jordan kept talking. I could see the slightest grin.

It was the last class of the day, and I had one thin, frayed nerve left intact. Slightly louder this time, "Jordan."

No response. Just more neighborly chitchat.

As my razor-thin nerve threatened to unravel, this exchange went on at least a half dozen times. Each time, my tone became edgier. I could feel myself getting red in the face. Kids side-eyed one another—this was getting good. Neither one of us was giving in, and I was supposed to be the one in control.

Sidney leaned toward me and whispered in a quiet, steady voice, "You're making it worse."

Whoa.

She was right. I gathered myself, took a deep breath, said a quick prayer for strength, and calmly asked the student next to Jordan to bring me their sketchbook. I smiled at Jordan as I asked, simultaneously and ever so slowly writing a zero next to his name in my grade book.

I opted for quiet, targeted action. I emailed his mom, who wholeheartedly agreed with my decision and informed him of his zero later that evening. As someone who never received zeros, Jordan was not happy.

(Side Note: Never underestimate the power of a perfectly timed parent email.)

The next day began with his apology. I graciously accepted, and that was the end of it. Never again would he ignore my request for his sketchbook. I'm fairly certain he shared his misfortune with his peers. I never received a late or incomplete sketchbook from anyone afterward.

Why are they compliant one day and defiant the next? I'm sure it's the hormones. Or the teenage drama. Or both.

Whatever it is, it has nothing to do with whether they *like* us.

It's tempting to wield power in a harsh manner. The frayed-teacher nerve is a real thing. The Enemy wants us to break, to crack under the pressure and blow up, and I was on the verge. These verses command us to speak without reproach in a dignified manner. Speech that is above reproach is the strongest defense we have when the Enemy threatens our teacher cool.

A graceful response is often difficult, especially when it comes to student insubordination. We can easily make a student's life miserable—just as I could have done with Jordan—an example for all to see. That's not a win for anyone. Who will see Jesus if you do that, if I do that? Student pushback is a given, and it will test the outer limits of our patience. As Jesus followers, we can choose a dignified response that is beyond reproach. When we wield authority with graceful words—especially when challenged—the Enemy is put to shame.

Rooted

The most effective model of graceful authority is God's still, small voice, and this voice is never cruel.

Refreshed

Reflect on a student interaction when God calmed your nerves and provided you with a perfectly dignified response.

3
Attentive

My son, if you will receive my words
And treasure my commandments within you,
Make your ear attentive to wisdom;
Incline your heart to understanding.

Proverbs 2:1–2

Teaching high school is not for the faint of heart.

Most days it feels like juggling flaming arrows in a circus with no ringleader to stop the show. Yeah, that's about right.

On my drive to work, I often begged God to cover me in his wisdom and patience.

I was about to encounter the teenage brain in action. God's provision was paramount in guiding my reactions, especially those prior to the appropriate amount of coffee on board.

There is no shortage of challenging moments. Bell to bell, anything can happen.

One day in the middle of my captivating art-history lecture, a student interrupted me mid-sentence. "Mrs. Fox, I have to call work and tell them I can come in tonight. Someone called off at the last minute. Can I go out in the hall and call my boss?"

Deep breath. Prayer for wisdom. "Of course. You are about to exercise your fabulousness by making your boss's job easier."

(Side Note: Being fabulous was the mindset and mission in our class.)

Upon returning—not even thirty seconds later—the young man leaned over to his neighbor and quickly scrawled the notes he'd missed while out in the hall. The work shift in question was covered, and somewhere a floor manager's stress level plummeted.

For a split second after his question, I'd thought my head would explode. How dare he interrupt my lecture! He was obviously texting his boss right in the middle of it!

After the deep breath and the prayer, it was as if I could hear God's still, small voice: *He could have called his boss in the middle of your lecture.* My initial thought was he ought to know better, but I could hear God reminding me that he is a teenage boy. And that he chose to ask first. *Celebrate the asking, my child, not the interruption.*

Fun fact: I had a kid call and order a pizza during my lecture once. Can you say, "Really deep breath?" Yeah. It's high school. Buckle up.

In the little everyday moments—major discipline issues notwithstanding—if we're being honest, are we inviting God's wisdom into every interaction, or are we inclining our hearts toward emotion and snap reflex?

As educators, success in our classrooms hinges on student understanding. It also hinges on understanding students. In the instance of my lecture interruption, it was a major win for that student to ask permission to step out of the room. I witnessed personal growth in the form of an ill-timed request.

Our students are still in the process of becoming thoughtful, responsible adults. God is not finished with them yet. When we see them in this formative light, remaining attentive in the moment to God's ever-present wisdom, the mid-lecture phone call isn't so bad after all. He is faithful to provide the perfect response to any ill-timed student request.

Proverbs 2:1–2 gives us four ways to approach God's wisdom: receive it, treasure it in our hearts, attend to it in all circumstances, and incline (lean in) to it. We have a responsibility as Jesus followers to demonstrate this wisdom in every action and reaction in our classrooms. We will face situations that tempt our reactions to the ragged edge of patience and grace. When we attend and lean in to God's direction, he steps in and covers our response, providing calm clarity in the moment. The young people in our care have the opportunity to see us respond in a godly manner to an otherwise challenging situation.

Rooted

God provides infinite wisdom for every response in our classrooms. His actionable steps are clear. We are to receive, treasure, attend, and incline our ear to his wisdom and understanding.

Refreshed

Reflect on a situation when your strained patience prompted you to rely on God's wisdom as you inclined your ear and responded to a classroom situation with grace.

4
Teachable

Trust in the Lord with all your heart
And do not lean on your own understanding.
In all your ways acknowledge Him,
And He will make your paths straight.

Proverbs 3:5–6

Parental support. Every teacher's secret weapon.

It's amazing. When it exists.

I had the privilege of teaching a talented young lady whose mother was her best friend—literally. Party friend, gossip friend, skip-school-to-go-shopping friend, host-of-the-coed-sleepover friend—you name it.

While seemingly every teenage girl's dream, the lack of parental guidance left this girl nervous, sad, and confused. This freedom led to crippling anxiety, which resulted in frequent absences.

When she did come to school, her fear of failure paralyzed her. Every new skill and concept was met with excessive whining and blatant avoidance. If you've ever had a talented, excessive whiner on your roster, you are tracking with me right now.

I made it my personal mission to get her excited about drawing. I pulled out all the stops, trying every foolproof method I could think of. If anyone could inspire her to create, it was me! I was like a magician at a kids' birthday party, yanking plastic flowers out of my hat and waiting for the thundering applause.

Her response?

Crickets.

One day after a particularly unproductive shading lesson, I was at my breaking point. "Listen. It's no secret you are insanely talented. The bigger question is, are you teachable? You can be the most talented person in the room, but if you're not willing to work hard, I can't do anything with you."

As I was speaking to her, I could hear God speaking to me.

You are a gifted teacher, but are you *teachable?*

My own strategies and valiant attempts had left him completely out of the equation. I was not trusting in him, and I was all up in my own understanding. In Proverbs 3:6 language, my path was twisted like a pretzel.

When faced with a roadblock, it's helpful to acknowledge God's wisdom and get specific about what we need. Enough of doing this our way. We need to trust him completely.

What if we asked, "What am I able to do with the resources you have provided?" In this case, he gently told me to remind her just how talented he had made her and how blessed I was to be a part of her journey. Instead of focusing on the work (or lack thereof), he shifted my focus to praise and acknowledging his placing her in my life.

It didn't happen overnight, but as the semester progressed, I noticed a change in both of us. Me, more gracious and encouraging; her, more teachable. She showed up several days in a row, then an entire week. I saw her beginning to believe in who she was made to be. God was working the kinks out of both our paths daily.

If we're not careful, we will seek answers from the wrong sources and focus on solutions outside of trusting God. In this case, I was relying solely on my teaching ability without giving any thought to the meeting place. This young lady needed to reboot her posture as a learner worthy of learning, just as we often need a reset when God is trying to teach us to trust him. He desires to meet us where we are, and he has something for us to learn with every student who enters our classroom. When we neglect his wisdom or seek answers from outside sources, our path in the classroom becomes difficult to navigate. When we call on God to fill us with his infinite wisdom, his strategies are always effective, and his timing is perfect. When we seek his wisdom first, he makes straight our path to meet students where they are.

Rooted

As Jesus followers, we can shift our angst to praise in any situation, acknowledging God first in every corner of our lives and watching him make our paths straight.

Refreshed

Reflect on a situation where a shift in focus from your ways to God's ways made the path straight.

5
Priority Shift

But seek first His kingdom and His righteousness,
and all these things will be provided to you.

Matthew 6:33

I've been accused of being wrapped a little tight.

Heck, I'm so tight that I squeak.

My saving grace here on earth?

Cardio.

At the start of my career, I put my morning workout first. Nothing happened before the workout. Once complete, it was off to work with barely enough time to grab a coffee before I hit the classroom door.

During my first year teaching, I could feel my stress level climbing, the waters rising. I was already a nervous wreck—new classroom, unfamiliar faces, no formal curriculum, tiny budget . . . you know the drill. As the year progressed, every little thing felt like a big deal.

After I'd landed my job, my daughter presented me with a jar full of handwritten Bible verses for my desk. She was sixteen years old, and her ability to know exactly how to encourage others was well beyond her years. At the end of a particularly stressful day, I pulled the first verse out of the jar and carefully unfolded it. In her beautiful handwriting it said, "Matthew 6:33." I looked it up. Hmmm. How fitting.

As much as I need cardio, I felt God saying I needed him more.

The next morning I started my day differently. I meditated on this verse and did some journaling. I laid my anxiety before him and spoke honestly about my struggles—everything from repeatedly tardy students (latte in hand) to repeated emails reminding me to take attendance. As I read the verse, I could hear him prompting me: *I have everything you need, and I'm right here trying to help you. Sit with me awhile.*

So I did. And as a result, that school day was noticeably different.

I made a choice to permanently change how I started each day. I shifted my schedule to include ten minutes with God prior to exercise.

After a few weeks, I saw a significant decrease in my stress level. It felt like a weight had physically been lifted from my shoulders. The situations were still the same—new everything, no experience, no budget—but the difference was a shift in my perception. Things just didn't seem like the big deal they once were.

I began to crave quiet time more than cardio. Ten minutes quickly turned to thirty and then to me rising even earlier so I could spend forty-five minutes with God.

Exercise became an afternoon or evening event. As a result, I saw an unexpected blessing. My sleep quality improved. If you're wrapped as tight as I am, you know just how amazing good sleep is.

I also began to see his hand in the smallest circumstances. As I spent more time in the Bible, I read over and over of the peace that comes to those who seek him first. As my priorities shifted, my peace grew.

When God tells us to "seek him first," we are to put him before all else. So often we wake up and go immediately to things that can never satisfy us. All the cardio in the world will only serve to wear me out. It cannot fill and refresh my soul.

God wants our priorities in alignment. He never intended for us to be wiped out. His intent has always been to go before us and do the heavy lifting. His promise in this verse is that "all things will be added" if we seek his kingdom and righteousness first. In order for this to occur, we may need to be honest with ourselves about who (or what) we seek first.

What a privilege to have the ability to spend time with God. To slow down and seek his righteousness. To see our struggles in a new light as we turn our face toward him. We can actually see "all things being added" when we realign our priorities and put him first.

Rooted

Heart strength embodies new meaning when we prioritize building our relationship with God.

Refreshed

Reflect on a time when you experienced renewed strength after prioritizing time in God's presence.

6
Trust

He will not fear bad news; His heart is steadfast, trusting in the Lord.

Psalm 112:7

Ever have one of those classes where you hold your breath when the tardy bell rings? That one class where any minute the train is going off the rails. Straight into the canyon.

One spring semester I had a class just like this. A spirited beginner drawing class. Twenty-five boys and six girls, mostly freshmen and sophomores. Throw in the misplaced senior counting down the days to graduation, and it was quite the behavior cocktail. You know the crew. To call it lively was an understatement.

I decided early on to approach the entire class with an elevated level of trust and respect. I addressed each student by their surname. I trusted them with more responsibility than other classes, and they earned their privileges by meeting a series of lofty expectations.

Whenever I wanted to get the attention of the entire class, I began with, "Beautiful people." If you want the undivided attention of an entire group of teenagers, try it—works every time.

One young man was always verbal about his distaste for the task at hand. When I greeted him, I was generally met with a guttural grunt. Combined with the daily potential for unrest, he could be quite the challenge.

Between the formal salutations and other creative behavior-management strategies, we were making decent progress. Until the day someone drove a utility truck into the traffic light in front of our school and the power went out.

This untimely outage happened at 2:05 p.m. School finished at 3:20. It was late May in North Carolina. Imagine thirty-four highly spirited teenagers in the last class of the day—no lights, no air conditioning, and no Wi-Fi. Yikes. Talk about bad news. The threat of chaos was real.

Fortunately, our room had a doorway to an outside courtyard.

Amid the rising murmur of unrest, I made my way to the front of the class, asking God for guidance with every step. "Beautiful people, as you know, we are without power. This leaves us with two options. We can stay inside and continue to work near the windows, or we can sit in the courtyard and peacefully enjoy the sunshine. I have full confidence that whichever option you choose, you will continue to be fabulous."

I'm not gonna lie—as I spoke, I had every one of my fingers crossed.

Half the class remained inside, while the other half made their way into the courtyard. As I couldn't be in both places at once, this gesture was either going to end miraculously or I was about to be out of a job.

As I was just hoping we would get to 3:05 without incident, the young man I mentioned earlier asked to speak to me in the hallway. Hmmm.

"Mrs. Fox, I know I can be a real pain in the butt [slight variation from the actual spoken name of the pain site]. I just want you to know that you have helped me become a better artist, and I'm sorry for giving you such a hard time."

Outside of thanking him, I was speechless. It was the first positive thing I had ever heard him say. I don't know if he had seen my crossed fingers or if my message of blind trust struck a chord. Maybe he finally saw himself as God sees him—trustworthy. Whatever it was, it was a light in the literal darkness.

I couldn't prevent the utility truck from derailing our class that day. In the face of potential chaos, my trust in God led to trusting my students. Not only did I have the privilege to see them step up, but I witnessed a personal breakthrough. All because the power went out.

Every unexpected event that brings bad news also brings with it an opportunity for renewed trust in our faithful God. There are times in our classrooms when we won't know how it will turn out, but we can be sure of one thing—God is with us in the moment. He promises us that a steadfast heart that trusts in the Lord will never fear bad news.

No matter the situation, we can trust God in the moment. We can also trust the people around us—even if those people are teenagers.

Rooted

Trust in the Lord even when the news seems bad. The news will not bring fear if your heart remains steadfast.

Refreshed

Reflect on a moment when bad news did not bring fear because your steadfast heart trusted in the Lord.

7
Sustained

Seek the Lord and His strength; seek His face continually.

1 Chronicles 16:11

I've been accused of being insensitive. Mostly by sensitive people.

Am I pragmatic? Yes.

Have I been emotionally broken by student life experiences—some of which I will never fully recover from? You bet I have.

Permanently.

For all the joy it brings, teaching can be gut wrenching. Over the course of my career, I have lived through things no one should have to experience. The funeral of a student found dead in a hotel room three thousand miles away from home. A fourteen-year-old out for the semester because they're in drug rehab for the second time. A young man found hanging in the backstage doorway of the auditorium. During school.

It took me eight months to type the rest of this devotion. Every time I attempted to delete it, God told me that someone needs to read it. Somewhere, his message of unconditional love is about to knock on the door of a heart.

In late March of 2016, I was preparing to go on a business trip with my husband. I had everything in order. The lessons were prepped, the substitute teacher was booked, the attendance roster printed.

As we were walking out the door, I received a frantic text from a former student. Something terrible had happened, and I had to call her immediately.

The news was devastating. One of the girls from our class had taken her own life the day before.

I was frozen. I had just seen this girl a few weeks earlier. She'd stopped by after school to visit. Nothing out of the ordinary. Just a visit.

The details were nothing short of horrific. I could barely breathe.

When we returned home, I went to see her parents. We sat in the living room as they told me what happened. How casual she was that day, saying she was going out to run an errand. As she left, her mom had thought, *That's odd. She never carries a purse.*

Thirty minutes later the phone rang. It was 3:30 p.m. Broad daylight.

The next day I returned to school. Walking into my classroom and seeing the table where she used to sit threatened my composure. I had given the day to God from the moment I opened my eyes.

As everyone took their seats, I stood at the front of the room. I spoke carefully as the tears made their way down my face. "As I'm sure you may have heard, we had a former student take her life last week. What you may not know is that she was also one of my students. I want you to listen carefully to what I'm about to say.

"I understand that being a teenager can be excruciating, because I've been one. I also know that life can seem hopeless, because I've felt it myself.

"If you can't find one person who you think cares about you, know this: Not only does your family care, but I care. I love each and every one of you more than you could ever know.

"And at the risk of losing my job, *God* loves you. His plan for your life is real and it is beautiful. You must promise me that removing yourself from the plan will never be an option under any circumstances."

By the time I finished, I wasn't the only one crying quietly. I honestly don't know how I made it through that speech or the days to follow. In a situation so confusing and senseless, God's presence and strength were the only things that sustained me.

As educators, difficult situations are all around us. Some of them are almost too much to bear. Today's verse commands us to seek God and his strength, as it is unmatched by human standards. The timeline for this seeking is very clear. It shall be continual.

Not knowing when the next unbearable circumstance will arise—and rest assured, it will—God's strength will prepare us for and carry us through anything. If we seek his face continually, we will be ready when the storms come.

That feeling of being carried through the fire is unmistakable. The body moves and the words come, but it is not by our own effort. It is 100 percent God sustaining us every moment.

Shortly after that difficult day, I found our class scrapbook. There was a handwritten note from the young lady who'd left us far too soon.

"Mrs. Fox, I'm not sure if there's a God, but I do know one thing. You took me in and treated me like one of your own, and I want to thank you for that."

Yes, my dear one, there is a God. And his sustaining power was the only thing that kept me going when you left.

Rooted

Seek the Lord in the darkest of circumstances, continually. He promises to sustain us.

Refreshed

Reflect on a time when you sought the Lord and he carried you through a dark and difficult time in the classroom.

8
Consider Today

So teach us to number our days, that we may present to You a heart of wisdom.

Psalm 90:12

In 2015 I had an AP Studio Art class of twenty-two girls—all seniors. Talk about an estrogen overload. Between the teen drama and the ever-present romance crises, most days I was in full-on counselor mode.

One day at the beginning of our journey toward portfolio submission, we launched into the subject of time. They were excited about senior year and so ready to graduate. I told them to slow down and enjoy each moment because life is both fast and precious. Even though it felt like graduation would never come, we would all blink and it would be May.

"Oh, come on Mrs. Fox—it's not gonna go *that* fast."

Looking back, none of us had any idea what the future held, and for that I am thankful.

The year was filled with many memorable moments. Art shows, gallery walks, local and regional competitions—a whirlwind of excitement. Our holiday class party was one for the books, complete with homemade treats and a class-wide gift exchange. I stumbled upon the party photos in my computer drive just the other day. Twenty-two beautiful ladies, their joy-filled eyes and their smiles bright under silly Santa hats.

The girls really came together in April, when my mother-in-law went into the hospital and I was out of town for almost two weeks. The day I returned, we still had more than fifty pieces of art to mat and frame.

I walked into the room, exhausted from the trip. There they were, excited to show me they had everything laid out assembly-line style. "It's all ready to go, Mrs. Fox—we just don't know how to use the mat cutter."

I instantly made a mental note for next year's class: *Train students on how to use the mat cutter*. Lesson learned.

It took us all afternoon, but we got everything framed, and the art show was a smashing success.

Then it happened. We blinked. There we were in early May, sitting with our paper portfolios, barcode stickers, and black pens.

I looked over at the young lady who thought it wouldn't go so fast, and there she was, clutching her portfolio with big tears in her eyes. "Oh my gosh, Mrs. Fox, you were right. It's over."

All that time spent anxiously waiting for submission day to hurry up and get here. To not realize the precious and fleeting nature of those days. What none of us knew at the time was that one of our beautiful twenty-two would tragically take her own life the following March.

Later, while processing this horrifying loss, I was reminded of the excitement of portfolio-submission day. At the time I had no idea how awful life was about to be on the heels of such an amazing year.

If you've experienced the loss of a student, you know how considering the gift of each day suddenly takes on a whole new meaning. God gives us beautiful days together as a class, learning, creating, and establishing a community. Let's remain focused and centered in the precious moments he affords. God's wisdom is found in deliberately experiencing joy in the moment instead of wishing the school year away.

Maybe he's telling us in this verse to consider each day because this consideration prepares us for the pain. I'm convinced that if we knew what lay ahead, the fear would surely paralyze us. If we take a minute to reflect, we can see how God carries us in every circumstance. He graciously affords us health and strength to relish the good times, and he provides indescribable comfort in the tragedy. It's wise for us to relish the time he gives us.

Rooted

For the moments ahead, God fortifies our souls. For what's behind, his loving-kindness provides us with the gift of remembering.

Refreshed

Reflect on a time when a situation, either good or bad, caused you to slow down and consider today, reflecting on God's faithfulness both past and present.

9
Bloom Where You're Planted

Blessed is the person who does not walk in the counsel of the wicked. . . .
He will be like a tree planted by streams of water,
Which yields its fruit in its season,
And its leaf does not wither;
And in whatever he does, he prospers.

Psalm 1:1, 3

Let's talk about talent.

I saw a quote today by a famous (*very* famous) author. "Talent is a dreadfully cheap commodity, cheaper than table salt. What separates the talented individual from the successful one is a lot of hard work."[1] If you've taught advanced art at the high school level, you'll be nodding all the way through this devotion. We've all experienced this scenario, and the frustration is exasperating.

One year I had a table of four students with raw talent. You know how it is—every time you walk by, you hear the *Hallelujah* chorus. There were three girls and one boy, and the boy's name was Matthew.

Matthew was a junior who had just left his family and friends in Brooklyn, New York, to move to North Carolina. The culture shift left him less than enthused with his new surroundings.

1. Stephen King, *Danse Macabre* (Scribner, 2010), 88.

His mother sent me a note telling me of his sour mood and adjustment struggles and that I needed to be prepared for both. She wasn't wrong. His effort level was a solid 45 percent.

I was a huge fan of bragging about my students to anyone who would listen, pointing out daily success and touting creative milestones as I saw them occur. If you were walking by my door, you were fair game for an impromptu gallery walk around my room. I'd even pulled the custodian in to show him how fabulous my students were.

None of this positive reinforcement resonated with Matthew, no matter what I said to him or about him.

There aren't many things that irritate me, but something that really grinds my gears is misuse or lack of use of God's gifts. Talent is a gift. Good health to use this talent is a gift. Freedom and opportunity are the gift icing on the cake. Shirking any of the aforementioned gifts raises my blood pressure significantly.

One day I was making my rounds, talking to various students about their progress. I approached Matthew's table to find his three tablemates hard at work as he slouched quietly, sulking and doodling.

I pulled up a chair and sat right next to him at the end of the table. My voice was quiet and my words steady. "You know, Matthew, sometimes we don't get to choose our location in life. Regardless of how we *feel*, we still have a choice to make. We will either wither away, or we will bloom where we're planted. I look forward to seeing your growth." I rose, pushed the chair in, and walked away.

Remember how I said it's difficult to watch students refuse to use their God-given talent? It's even more difficult when we do it ourselves. As I'm thinking about Matthew, I'm sitting at my desk, writing a devotion that should have been written six months ago. Instead I was sulking and doodling. It's humbling to see the words on the screen in front of me.

God uses people to fulfill his plans. He had planted Matthew, full of talent, at that table in my classroom so he could recognize his own potential. God has planted me here in South Carolina, in a personal wilderness where he spoke truth into my next assignment. It was here that he revealed the talent and opportunity before me, regardless of where I thought I would rather be.

Very often our plans are not God's plans. When we choose to stop sulking and listen for his direction, we clear the path for growth. For a life planted by the stream of living waters that never stop flowing. A life that yields to him, which then yields abundant fruit in due seasons.

Fast-forward to six months ago, when I received a beautiful message from Matthew, all the way from Florence, Italy. He is in his final year of industrial design, in full bloom as an apprentice to a third-generation cobbler in Florence.

No more sulking. No more doodling. Just prosperous fruit for us both. Him designing handcrafted shoes and me spending time here with you, fulfilling God's call.

Rooted

Remain confident in your current season, knowing that God is nurturing your growth every step of the way.

Refreshed

Reflect on a time in your life when you couldn't make sense of the season, but with God's help you grew into full bloom.

10
Consider One Another

Make my joy complete by being of the same mind, maintaining the same love, united in spirit, intent on one purpose. Do nothing from selfishness or empty conceit, but with humility consider one another as more important than yourselves; do not merely look out for your own personal interests, but also for the interests of others.

Philippians 2:2–4

Student behavior can be difficult to assess and even more difficult to manage.

Thirty-plus personalities all in one place, half of them wishing they were somewhere else. Bringing the group together is important for successful classroom management. And unifying any class requires a common mission, with everyone headed in the same direction.

Our classroom mindset was one based on excellence. My mantra from day one was that everyone is capable of learning any skill, concept, or technique set before them. Daily effort toward this goal was necessary. We had our own name for this goal—"fabulousness."

Every student had a personal responsibility to consider their own actions as either helping or hindering others in their quest for fabulousness. The focus was not so much how their behavior affected them personally, but how it affected their fellow classmates—and me.

We spent time at the beginning of the semester learning how to wait. This is often difficult for young people.

Hard to believe, right?

Instant gratification is today's norm, experienced daily on every social media platform. To wait quietly, without a phone and only one's thoughts, can seem like an impossible task.

We always took a baseline skills test the first week of school. It gave me the information I needed to effectively structure my curriculum. Because it was our first written test as a group, students often wanted to know if they could be on their phones when they were finished.

The answer was a nonnegotiable "No."

After the look of shock and disbelief wore off, I explained it this way. "We are a newly established family who seeks the fabulousness of others. Our family members need time to finish in a focused environment. The distraction of clicking, scrolling, and giggling at videos and texts hinders the progress of those around us."

It always amazed me how the lightbulb in their heads instantly illuminated when I delivered the explanation this way. You'd think that they would be irritated by the "no." Instead it was, "Ohhhh, okay, that makes sense."

Teenagers often get a bad rap. People say they're self-absorbed and thoughtless, and maybe some are. The real question is, *Why*? They aren't born this way. At the core of the human spirit is a willingness to help. The simple explanation of their role in another person's success is sometimes all they need to "get it."

This no-phone policy held an unexpected bonus. Because playing on their phones after finishing was not an option, students had no reason to hurry up and finish. As a result, they spent more time and effort on the baseline. I wish I could tell you I'd planned it this way, but I cannot. I simply wanted them to see how good it feels to put someone else's needs before their own.

In today's Scripture passage, Paul gives us God's beautiful directive on how to achieve unity with one simple thought: This life is not all about us. Our personal mission should be placing the needs of others before our own. In the case of our baseline test, instead of our own phone time, we learn to wait on others and to offer them a chance to succeed.

There were thirty people in the classroom. When we focused our energy inward, only one person succeeded. When each person focused on the needs of the other twenty-nine, everyone succeeded.

Putting others first is God's original design. Christ's journey to the cross is the blueprint of humility, as he placed our need for salvation above his need to live. He willingly gave his life for us in order to free us from an eternity separated from him. Once we show our students how to reposition their focus outward, a unified classroom begins to takes shape.

The end result is a roomful of givers, not takers. Filled with a joy that is complete, maintaining the same love, united in spirit, intent on one purpose. Fabulousness.

Rooted

God's selfless love for us is the perfect model for an outward focus on classroom management. A room filled with selfless intent leads to a classroom with a unified spirit.

Refreshed

Reflect on an inspiring moment in your own classroom when you witnessed students selflessly put the needs of others before their own.

11
Counselor

For a Child will be born to us, a Son will be given to us; and the government will rest on His shoulders; and His name will be called Wonderful Counselor, Mighty God, Eternal Father, Prince of Peace.

Isaiah 9:6

Imagine with me a world in which all we do is teach educational content from 8:00 a.m. to 3:00 p.m. nine months of the year.

The other three months we're lying by the pool, thinking about everything but school. This is how most people view our profession.

How many times I have heard, "But you only work nine months." Every time I hear it, I get an overwhelming urge to retaliate in an unkind manner.

You get it, because you've heard it too.

Oh, how I wish teaching was all that was required. We also get to perform the duties of counselor, negotiator, mediator, and constant motivator, just to name a few. At the high school level, the role of counselor is a given. We can expect a daily onslaught of raw emotions.

Yes, daily.

When students arrived upset, my first question was, "Is it parents, grades, friends, or a love interest?" My second question was, "Is there anything I can do to help?"

There were times when students confided in me, and the answer to that first question was heavy with regret. A life-altering decision had left their world crumbling.

One morning during my first year teaching, a beautiful girl walked into my room and burst into tears. The emotion was so raw and the tears so loud that I could barely get my first question out. As the class filed in, the students could see that something was terribly wrong.

I got the class on task and took her into the hall, to find out she was pregnant. Sixteen years old. Her boyfriend was seventeen. Her father wanted her to have an abortion. She and her boyfriend wanted to keep the baby, graduate, and get married. She was inconsolable, caught between parental authority and impending parenthood.

She spent the better part of the day in my room, crying through each of my classes. We had a long conversation about choices. Life is one choice after another, from hitting the snooze button to having unprotected sex. And each one comes with a consequence.

She kept asking me what she should do. I, as her teacher, did not have the authority to tell her how to proceed. What I did tell her was to consider the remainder of her years on the planet. There would be many years ahead. I asked her to imagine how they would look and feel once her decision was final. And then move forward from there.

I felt God telling me that this job was so much more than teaching, and that in order to cope and provide wise counsel, I needed to stay close to Jesus.

Thirteen years ago, during that tearful conversation, I had no idea how things would turn out. It's difficult to know what to say, especially when lives and futures are at stake. It's tempting to proceed in our own thoughts and opinions. We're adults, right? We should have all the answers for our students.

Quite frankly, I was terrified. How blessed we are to call on our Eternal Counselor in pivotal moments like this. Thankfully, he always provides the right words. We can rest knowing he will guide us in helping our students, no matter the issue. He is waiting to help us—all we have to do is invite him into the conversation.

God's title in Isaiah 9:6 is Wonderful Counselor. In Hebrew, this title is *Pele Yoetz*—meaning "Miraculous Adviser."[2] We've all experienced classroom situations where God provided wonderful counsel and miraculous advice.

2. "One God, Many Names," Jewish Jewels, December 1, 2023, https://www.jewishjewels.org/news-letters/one-god-many-names/.

Rather than shy away from a difficult conversation, we are able to lean on our Heavenly Adviser for the next steps. Even if all we offer is a compassionate ear, listening to our students with grace is often the wisest counsel of all.

I saw a post on Facebook recently—family photos taken in a field filled with wildflowers. There she was, that sixteen year-old-girl, now a wife and mother, years away from that life-changing decision. Seated in front of her and her husband were two beautiful girls, all smiles, the warm sun on their shoulders.

Rooted

This profession reaches far beyond instruction. When the job calls for us to take on additional roles, the wonderful counsel and miraculous advice of the Holy Spirit is at our disposal.

Refreshed

Reflect on a difficult conversation with a student in which you invited God into the moment and he filled your responses with his miraculous advice.

12
Weight-Lifting Words

Anxiety in a person's heart weighs it down,
But a good word makes it glad.

Proverbs 12:25

Many students enter our classroom outwardly anxious and afraid. We see them as disengaged, checked out, and full of behavior problems that threaten to sink our ship.

I'm gonna go out on a limb and make a bold statement. Ninety-nine percent of the time, these behaviors have nothing to do with how they feel about us or our classes.

Yeah, it's easier to internalize their actions and make it all about us. They hate us, or they hate our class, or both. Seriously? Do we honestly fancy ourselves as that important in the lives of our students that our teaching is the driving force in their behavior?

While not as simple, the challenge is to meet them where they are and show them their worth, regardless of how we perceive their actions.

I had a young lady in my fall drawing class who was so anxious that she could barely speak. From the moment I met her, her eyes were filled with fear. Most days she would sit at her table, head in her hands, doing nothing. To make matters worse, from the little drawing she had done, she was amazingly talented.

In the beginning of the semester, I was unsure if this fear was real or an excuse not to work. There I was, internalizing her behavior. A few days later, the notes began to appear on my desk at the end of class. Folded carefully and filled with remorse for her lack of progress. They were difficult to read. She wanted to work, but the fear paralyzed her.

We were in the middle of a really intense pencil drawing—the assignment was to draw a pile of shoes. After three days of no pencil on the paper and repeated notes on my desk, I asked her to stay after class so we could chat.

Rather than ask her what was causing the fear, I simply asked her if she could wave a wand and use her amazing ability to draw anything she wanted, what would she be comfortable drawing? Her eyes lit up, and she showed me a doodle of a Furby. I had never seen one before, and while the little stuffed creature was not part of the assignment, he was pretty darn cute. I had noticed that she spent a lot of time doodling this character, and what I saw in this moment was the light in her eyes.

"Then you, my dear, are going to draw your Furby."

It was as if a three-hundred-pound weight was lifted off her shoulders. She stood up straight (she had a habit of standing with her head down), smiled (for the first time), and promised she would return to class tomorrow with her reference photo, ready to work.

She arrived the next morning with a picture of not just one Furby, but two. They were leaning into each other, facing the camera, side by side. Our class was ninety minutes long. She drew with focused intent the entire time and left without leaving a note.

The rest of the semester was not always as productive, and as it progressed, some days the anxiety was just too much. She never revealed the source of the fear, but that wasn't important. I was learning as much from her as she was from me. I had been asking God to give me wisdom on how to help her. There's a fine line between not wanting to do the work and not being able to do the work. My pride could have easily taken over, forcing her to draw the shoes. God's guidance instead was for me to put my pride and agenda aside and help her cope with the anxiety. He then provided the words to lift the weight.

When we seek the Lord's guidance for carefully chosen words, he will provide the right words along with their timeliness. Uplifting words of affirmation that enable student progress in the face of crippling angst.

This verse is clear about the power of our words. An anxious heart is heavy, filled with emotions that are difficult to carry. A word can lift the weight from a heart and make it glad. When we cry out to God from our own place of anxiety, he reminds us in his still, small voice who we are—chosen, worthy, and loved. Restorative weight-lifting words from our Father.

Rooted

For students burdened with anxiety, we can provide good words that remove the weight and make their anxious hearts glad—just as our heavenly Father does for us.

Refreshed

Reflect on ways you've received words that lifted your anxiety and made your heart glad.

13
Gratitude

Therefore, since we receive a kingdom which cannot be shaken, let's show gratitude, by which we may offer to God an acceptable service with reverence and awe.

Hebrews 12:28

"It's a fast life."

It's also a fast semester.

We've all felt the push to cram all the information possible into an eighteen-week course.

Our semester always ended with an art-history exam, given college-survey style via a 120-slide PowerPoint. It was a truckload of information delivered in a whirlwind of presentations, flash cards, and notes.

Let's back up to the beginning of the semester, when I often heard every teacher's favorite question: "Why do we have to learn this?"

Good questions deserve better answers.

"Because it's cool to know stuff. One day in the future you're going to be out and about, experiencing this beautiful world and all it has to offer. The chance of you seeing art is extremely high. I want you to return to this moment and think, 'Hey, I've seen this. Mrs. Fox made us learn about this.' Maybe you'll even look me up online and send me a note."

(Side Note: I recently received a Facebook message from a former student who saw a work by Robert Rauschenberg in Europe. She thanked me for the learning, even though she didn't appreciate it at the time. (I can still see her taking notes with exaggerated boredom.) The message was a truly glorious teacher moment (we've all had them). They make the job worthwhile.

On final exam day, I always found myself in a place of overwhelming gratitude.

The cover slide of the exam presentation was always our class picture. Taken the first week of school, eighteen weeks prior to this day. Projected large and bright on the screen, it never failed to bring a series of gasps and giggles. Tans had faded and hairstyles had changed, but one thing remained constant: We were a unique group, frozen in time, and we would never be here, like this, in this exact place ever again.

I liked to give a little speech right before the exam started. "I'm gonna try hard to say this without crying. It has been a distinct privilege to be your teacher. I have thoroughly enjoyed getting to know each and every one of you. If I never see you again, or if I see you next semester, I want you to hear me. In this life there are no mistakes. We are all here for a reason, and God has a specific plan for you and the rest of your life. Now let's crush this exam!"

What a gift. The kingdom of God is literally sitting in front of us every day for eighteen weeks. A field of ministry before our eyes. Because God has given us a vital role to play in the lives of these students, we are commanded to show gratitude toward him with reverence and awe. And not just to God but to our students as well. How can we possibly know the world-changers who may be sitting in our midst? The next Nobel Peace Prize winner may very well be in the third row, two seats from the front. Only God knows their paths, and he has blessed us with their presence along the journey. We can express genuine gratitude for our time spent together. A sincere note of verbal thankfulness is something they don't hear every day.

Inside our classrooms, we are all part of God's unshakeable kingdom. No matter who we teach, the wonder is found in our opportunity to know every student. Our God is a God of plan and purpose. The awe is found in why he appointed us to meet in the first place.

While the details may remain a mystery, we can be grateful for this truth: Every student in the room is present for a divine appointment in time, part of an eternal kingdom that cannot be shaken.

Rooted

Center your heart on gratitude resulting from God's unshakeable and perfectly appointed members of his kingdom in your classroom.

Refreshed

Reflect on a time when you felt overwhelming gratitude for your students and made it a point to tell them in person.

14
A Great Distance

As far as the east is from the west, so far has He removed our wrongdoings from us.

Psalm 103:12

Relationships can be difficult.

Teachers are in the relationship-building business, constantly striving for strong, trustworthy relationships with our students.

I don't have to tell you that some relationships are easier to build than others.

I used to see it like this: "If you're nice to me, I'll be nice to you." As if the teacher-student dynamic hinges on how kids feel about us at any given moment.

Hilarious.

I once heard a veteran teacher say, "Kids have a crap meter." In other words, they know when you genuinely care about them.

As I type this, a spirited young lady named Sara comes to mind. If she wasn't in the principal's office, she was in a parent-teacher conference or the back of a squad car. When her name showed up on your roster, you'd better buckle up.

As luck would have it, one semester her name showed up on my roster. At least two coworkers informed me how horrifying my semester was about to be.

Sara walked into my room on the first day of school ready for a fight. By the end of the first week, she was ready to work. If you're expecting a behavior-management miracle story, you can exhale. Sara's attitude readjustment was a natural response to a forgiveness approach.

My students' first impression of me was pretty blunt and completely devoid of fancy behavior strategies. "Your past behavior prior to entering my classroom is irrelevant. My mantra is, 'Your history will not determine how I see you. Today is a new day, and the past is the past. We are all here to be fabulous, because in this classroom, you are fabulous.'"

That went for Sara too.

Something strange happens when students realize they don't have to live up to their reputation, either good or bad. Maintaining either position can be exhausting.

Even though I operated my classroom on a new-day mantra, situations and people still have the propensity to become unhinged.

It's high school. Buckle up.

A month into the semester, I was notified that Sara would be out on a ten-day suspension. Evidently she had been caught in some messy and undignified conflict resolution with another student. She faced expulsion if found on school grounds under any circumstances.

On the first day of her suspension, she came bouncing into my room at 3:30 p.m. "Mrs. Fox! I came to get my project!"

She didn't care about getting expelled. She knew that I cared about her success, and in spite of her untimely alienation, she knew there was no judgment on my part—my focus was her success.

I could have called the office and she would have been expelled. In her case, it probably would have been the end of her high school career. Right or wrong, I didn't turn her in.

She returned nine days later with a beautiful drawing and a calmer approach to those around her. Who knows—maybe it was me not calling the office that readjusted her attitude. Whatever it was, grace carried the situation.

As Jesus followers, we have the perfect model for forgiveness to pass on to others. Our actions did not prevent Jesus from reaching across the divide to offer us eternal salvation. In fact, he loved us in spite of our actions. This verse tells us that our wrongdoings are as far apart from who we are as the east is from the west. Maybe he paints this picture of a vast distance so we won't attempt to retrieve them. In his eyes they are no longer seen.

If we want our students to see Jesus in our actions, the common denominator must always be grace. God has removed our wrongdoings from us. This is a picture of how we should view our students, who are navigating home life, school, friends, social media, acceptance, and rejection. We can approach them by placing a great distance between their wrongdoings and who they are. Christ forgives us equally because what we do is not who we are.

Rooted

Approach student wrongdoings as God approaches us, separating what we do from who we are with a great distance—as far as the east is from the west.

Refreshed

Reflect on a time when you separated the action from the person and extended divine forgiveness.

15
Counselors in Our Midst

Without consultation, plans are frustrated,
But with many counselors they succeed.

Proverbs 15:22

Feedback is invaluable.

Asking for it can be terrifying, especially from our students.

I decided early on that as scary as it was to ask (mostly due to the teenage no-filter factor), if I was going to serve students well, their feedback was critical.

At the end of the semester on final exam day, students filled out a course evaluation. They answered a series of questions, reflecting on everything from procedures to project choices to choice of background music. Every student was required to complete the evaluation—no exceptions.

This handwritten evaluation was always completed on final exam day. A little backstory is in order. Some of the feedback ended up in my syllabus presentation during week one of the next semester. This feedback informed incoming students of what to expect in my class. Students sit up and take notice when information is delivered by their peers.

You may be wondering, with the advent of Google Forms, why the students didn't complete this evaluation on the computer. What's with the handwriting?

The answer is both simple and a bit selfish. Handwriting tells a unique individual story. Some script is neat and calculated, slanted and perfectly spaced. Some script is jagged and disjointed, rising and falling in waves across the paper.

As I read and reflect on each answer, I can hear each student's voice as clear as if they were reading it aloud.

Sitting alone, walls clean and chairs up, I was both sad and encouraged. I was sad that the students had gone and encouraged by the feedback left behind. They'd written about everything from their enhanced art skills to the atmosphere of solace in the room.

Reflections on everything from improving procedures to storing supplies. The students brought things to my attention that my busyness and exhaustion had caused me to never realize or overlook completely. Some comments focused solely on the free lollipops, and those also brought a sweet boost of encouragement. Some ideas were so practical and simple that I remember thinking, "Why didn't I think of that?" See the second sentence of this paragraph. Exhaustion can seriously fog the brain.

Every sentence delivered support from many counselors. The people who knew best how to describe the effectiveness of my teaching methods—my students.

Each semester ran smoother and became easier to navigate as the years passed and the course evaluations multiplied.

I love how this verse says that "plans" with "many counselors" succeed. It's teacher language, plain as day, right there in Proverbs. Planning is the foundation of our profession. Coming alongside our students and including them in our process offers them genuine investment in our classrooms. They feel seen and heard, and our interest in their opinions tells them how we view them—as worthy.

God provides teachers with a built-in source of counselors to assist them in their professional growth. Our initial thought may be that the students will see this as a chance to be crass or snarky. And yes, they are young people, so we may receive a boneheaded response from time to time. But overall it was my experience that once they realized the value placed on their input, the snarky feedback was almost nonexistent.

What if our students aren't merely recipients of educational content—what if they are actually counselors in our midst with an important role to play in the success of our plans? When we value their feedback, we have the opportunity to experience growth.

God's Word tells us that without consultation, plans are frustrated. Frustration is exhausting, and searching in the wrong places is frustrating. Instead of searching for answers online or in the neighboring classroom, we can start with the thirty-plus counselors God has placed right in front of us.

Rooted

Our classrooms are filled with counselors. Seek their counsel, for with it comes plans filled with success.

Refreshed

Reflect on a time when you received feedback from students that revolutionized your teaching practice.

16
Consistent

Every good thing given and every perfect gift is from above, coming down from the Father of lights, with whom there is no variation or shifting shadow.

James 1:17

Ever arrived at someone's house not knowing how you will be received? You could be met with anything from a joyous welcome to a prickly reception. Either your experience there will be amazingly fabulous, or your entire day is about to downshift significantly.

For many students, this is their daily experience in the classroom. They arrive at school each day anxiously anticipating the mood (and subsequent fall-out) of the teacher behind the door.

When I was in fifth grade, I spent 180 days with a teacher who suffered manic, unpredictable mood swings. How I (or anyone else in the room) learned anything I will never know. Looking back, I'm sure there were intense personal issues at play. Regardless of the reason, we were all tiptoeing across a classroom full of razor-sharp eggshells.

Life is full of circumstances that are often unchosen. How we decide to act and react determines our effectiveness on those around us.

When students enter a classroom rooted in consistency, they know what to expect—no surprises. The mood is even. The atmosphere is calm. The harvest is ripe for learning. There is no anxiety in this place because expectations and procedures are firmly established. Most people don't generally care for unpleasant surprises, and students are no different.

I'm not saying things won't go off the rails. This is education. The train has a way of veering off the track. The fire alarm will sound in the middle of the final exam. The hallway brawl will break out just as we're about to begin the lesson. The power will go out. But when the outside forces threaten derailment—and they will—consistency will set the train back on course.

On a personal note, how will we receive students into our classrooms in the face of our own personal trials? I have taught through some harrowing circumstances, as I'm sure you have too. Regardless of our situation, the bell still rings, bringing the students with it, no matter what's happening in our lives behind the scenes.

Students can often sense when we are having a bad day. Consistency in procedures is important, but what if we covered our personal lives with the unwavering light of our heavenly Father? We can decide to immerse ourselves in God's unchanging presence and choose a mood that meets students with a joyous welcome in spite of our circumstances. A welcome that washes our classrooms in his glorious light.

"Mrs. Fox, why are you always in a good mood?"

"When I'm here in this classroom, I am surrounded by blessings. I'm here with my fabulous people, watching them do remarkable things. Nothing else matters."

While we are humanly incapable of perfect consistency, we have the perfect model of the One who is. By his grace and indwelling Spirit, we can strive toward stability, knowing that the shadow never shifts. God's light source is always the same—the shadow it casts never shifts. We enter our classrooms each day knowing that he is in control, and no matter what that day brings, his wisdom and love never shift. As we rely on a God whose character never changes, we can offer our students a consistent classroom able to withstand a shifting world.

As we welcome our students, let's take comfort in the opportunity to provide a place they never need to be nervous to enter. For a great many students, our classrooms are the only safety they know. As we emulate the consistent light of our God, let's offer them a welcoming safety capable of illuminating their world.

Rooted

As we enter God's holy presence, we never need to be concerned with whom we will meet. His unchanging character and mood are always welcoming.

Refreshed

Reflect on an area in your life that has impacted your consistency, and ask our unwavering God for direction.

17
God's Workmanship

For we are His workmanship, created in Christ Jesus for good works, which God prepared beforehand so that we would walk in them.

Ephesians 2:10

The first day of school.

Freshly waxed floors welcoming two-thousand teenagers back to the scene of learning.

I can still see everyone sitting at the clean tables.

New clothes, new backpacks, half-asleep from waking up before 11:00 a.m.

Every student in the room is keeping a divine appointment, as am I.

One of two things was guaranteed to happen with every appointment. Either the student received a blessing, or I did.

Most of the time it was both.

Our journey began with me celebrating their presence on my roster—God's initial divine appointment. Not by informing them of the limited amount of bathroom trips or our late grade policy. Not that procedures aren't important—of course they are—but today was dedicated purely to the value of their presence.

The first day in my classes was always about learning every student's name (yep, everyone's name, in one class period). My first trip down the roster, learning each preferred name and saying it with corrected pronunciation, cemented the first bricks in our class foundation.

It sounds like a small gesture, learning someone's name, but to the students, it spoke volumes. The message was clear—who you are matters, and I want to know who you are before we learn anything about art.

Their shock and awe always made me smile. As I went around the room one by one, saying their names over and over, laughing when I would forget a name and have to say, "Wait . . . Help me . . . Help me . . . I can't remember!" The levity helped to relieve the tension for the people who'd entered thinking they were stuck here for eighteen weeks.

My day-one goal was to take them from "I'm stuck here" and transform their perception to "I can't wait to get back here tomorrow."

We are literally God's workmanship. His plan for us began as he formed us in our mother's womb. We are created purposefully, with various gifts and talents, all of which are intended for good works. For educators, it's not only about the teaching—we are designed with the gift of nurturing others toward personal success. How exciting for us to know these young people at this time in their lives. We could be in the presence of future greatness without knowing it.

The journey to good works begins with celebrating our students' presence on our rosters—this is the initial divine appointment. Just the fact that each student is carefully placed in our classrooms means God has something big planned for all of us. This group of God's workmanship has been brought together on purpose.

We share a common vision for every student in every class: to help them discover their endless potential as God's intentional workmanship, created to do their good works, not good works intended for their neighbor. Not only is this true for our students, but it's also true for us. We are God's deliberate design, our entire being created with purpose for this exact classroom. Not the classroom down the hall, not the classroom we left (voluntarily or not) to work at this new school. Comparison to how God created others, and their position or purpose, has no place in our present situation. He designs us to walk in our own good works, not someone else's.

When we survey our rosters, we can see God's handiwork in human form, destined for good works. Let's lead these young people with purpose, calling on every God-given ability and trait we possess to do the job well. Their design (and ours) is already complete. All that's left is a steady walk toward success, trusting the Designer we know is perfect.

Rooted

Celebrate God's perfect plan and purpose for yourself and every student in your classroom. We are all his deliberate workmanship. Good works are on the way.

Refreshed

Reflect on a time when you witnessed a student realize their potential as God revealed the intent of his workmanship in their young life.

18
A Brand-New Day

As far as the east is from the west, so far has He removed our transgressions from us.

Psalm 103:12

It's easier to be sick at school than to prepare for a substitute.

Preach it, Tiff.

In my first year of teaching, I had a district-level administrator observe me once a week. It just so happened he was scheduled for a day when I was returning to school after having a substitute for two days. Cue the anxiety.

Upon arrival at school, I was met with a lengthy note from my substitute. Every teacher's nightmare: the note that fills the page and has a list of names at the end. Ugh.

Let's just say, several young men had made some questionable behavior choices while the substitute was in charge. The class in question was my last of the day. During lunch I had written the proper referrals, called parents, and spoken with my principal.

(Side Note: Who needs to eat lunch anyway, right?)

The young men in question had already been to the main office prior to class.

The last class of the day finally arrived. The moment of reckoning was upon us. Right before the bell rang, I briefly explained the shenanigans to the district administrator. He settled in with his clipboard, and I could tell he was curious how I would handle the situation.

As always, I welcomed the class, told them how much I missed them while I was away, and delivered our learning goals for the day. Waiting for the lecture and obviously confused by its absence, the class worked on their drawings.

One gentlemen involved in the substitute shenanigans nervously raised his hand. "Mrs. Fox, aren't you going to yell at us for actin' like fools while you were gone?"

"Why would I do that? That was yesterday. Consequences related to yesterday have been administered to all parties involved. Today is a brand-new day. Today I am confident you are all ready to be fabulous."

Oftentimes the exhausting demands of teaching bring our patience to the breaking point. There are some students who are intuitively adept at pushing buttons, especially those of a substitute teacher.

In the midst of being pushed, I am reminded of how God sees my own disobedience. Thankfully, he doesn't hold a grudge. Natural consequences are often unavoidable, but he still forgives me and welcomes me with open arms.

In this case, the rest of the students witnessed forgiveness and had the chance to see what grace in action looked like.

The administrator watched as the young men apologized to me in front of the entire class. In my evaluation he said, "I've been in education for thirty years. I've never seen discipline handled so graciously or so effectively."

Consequences are always in order for bad behavior choices in the classroom. Everything we do from a leadership stance sends a message to our students. Allowing disrespect of any kind (toward anyone) will eat away at the fabric of our classroom community. Write the referrals, call the parents, and notify administration.

Then move on.

Rather than write a student off permanently or harbor a grudge, we can take a page from God's playbook and move forward with a clean slate. Thank goodness he doesn't hold us accountable with our lives for our transgressions. On the contrary, he tells us that our transgressions are as far removed from us as the east is from the west. When we address unacceptable student behavior with public forgiveness, students experience grace based on who they are, not what they've done. This is exactly how our loving Father handles our transgressions.

The consequences remain, but his attitude toward us is unchanged. He is just as committed to our well-being and success now as prior to the infraction.

Rooted

God's approach is always the most effective approach. Forgive student transgressions as God forgave you, separating the sin from the person, knowing that today is a brand-new day.

Refreshed

Reflect on a time in your life when you extended unmerited forgiveness or received it from someone else. In either case, it's a glorious feeling.

19
Do the Work

Whatever you do, do your work heartily, as for the Lord and not for people.

Colossians 3:23

Somewhere along the line, hard work got a bad rap.

Teenagers can spend an endless amount of energy avoiding hard work.

The ability to work hard is a picture of God's grace. The breath in our lungs, our freedom to attend school and learn, is not a given—it's a gift. Even in the midst of good health and educational freedom, not everyone is destined for higher learning.

I often saw students graduate and go on to big colleges, only to see them back home permanently in January after failing the first semester.

My favorite college advice to students was this: "*Getting* into college is one thing . . . *staying* in college is another thing altogether." I remember my own college orientation almost forty years ago. The dean said, "Look around. Only one in four of you will still be here in four years."

I was privileged to teach a precious young lady with cognitive disabilities. She came in each day, smiling and ready to work hard. While she would never work above a second-grade level, the sincere effort she brought to our classroom was refreshing and evident to everyone who knew her.

She heard everyone around her saying that if you worked hard, you could go to college. I had many conversations with her mom, who had the heartbreaking task of telling her daughter that college would not be in her future.

In January that same year, I ran into a former student who had failed out of college after one semester. He was insanely talented and intelligent. Unfortunately, his social calendar had consumed most of his semester, resulting in a nearly nonexistent GPA.

Shortly after I saw him, I was telling my students his story (in a generic way), hoping to capitalize on every teachable moment of studying more and socializing less.

I was stopped midsentence by the young lady I mentioned above. She looked up from her work and asked, "Mrs. Fox, why didn't he just do the work?"

The question hung in the air for all to ponder. More than one student had a "wow" look on their face.

"I don't know."

Lame as it was, it was all I could come up with. In my heart of hearts, I knew that young man thought the hard work was secondary to the excitement of college life. I also knew that this young lady wanted very badly what he'd carelessly thrown away.

Her steadfast work ethic reminds me of this verse. She doesn't know it, but she forever changed the way I view the concept of work. One conversation transformed my petty annoyances into a fresh appreciation for the opportunity to work hard regardless of the task. In moments like this, God is speaking through his children, sending a message we need not miss.

How blessed are we? God has handed us the opportunity to make our own way. When we decide to work heartily for him, we honor this gift. Working hard even in the mundane glorifies his name. He equipped us with physical cognitive ability and then carefully placed us in a position to demonstrate the value of these blessings. Our work is a testimony of thanksgiving to our generous Father.

How wonderful to show our students the value of the ability to work—even when the work is mundane and boring—with our God-given physical capacities. Something as menial as washing paint palettes and wiping down tables takes on new purpose when committed to the Lord. When we work alongside our students, we celebrate what a gift it is to be able to clean up in the first place.

Rooted

Whatever the task, exciting or mundane, approach it heartily, working only for God's glory. He has given us good health, freedom, and opportunity to work hard.

Refreshed

Reflect on a task that you once viewed as burdensome, but that God shifted your perspective, revealing the gift of being able to perform it.

20
Continual Prayers

With every prayer and request, pray at all times in the Spirit, and with this in view, be alert with all perseverance and every request for all the saints, and pray in my behalf, that speech may be given to me in the opening of my mouth, to make known with boldness the mystery of the gospel, for which I am an ambassador in chains; that in proclaiming it I may speak boldly, as I ought to speak.

Ephesians 6:18–20

A teacher's drive to school can be full of what-ifs.

What if there's a hallway throwdown during homeroom? What if we have to hide from an active shooter during lunch? And a thousand what-ifs in between.

Yet we return each day, dedicated and focused on our mission to help young people.

During my student-teaching experience, I started a habit of praying for my students as I drove to school. Not only did the prayers help to calm my nerves, but they also set my focus where it belonged—on the people God had so graciously placed in my care. When I was finally blessed with my own classroom, I made sure to continue this habit.

As I drove, I would say their names aloud, one by one, asking the Lord to flood each person with everything they needed for the challenges of the day ahead. I prayed for their home life. I prayed for their safety on their way to school. I prayed for their success once they arrived. I could feel God's presence fill me with every name I spoke. I could also feel the anxiety subside as my focus shifted outward.

I also prayed for God's wisdom, words, and provision for every moment and encounter I was about to face. Remember, I was speaking all this out loud, and the windows were down if the weather was good.

This was way before hands-free Bluetooth. People in the surrounding cars must have thought I was nuts.

Once at school, the peace I felt walking into the classroom was unexplainable. If the school day went off the rails—and sometimes it did—God always provided a solution, a resolution, or an answer. Always. I had the words I needed for every interaction—pleasant or unpleasant. God's provision was abundant at every turn.

God tells us in this verse to pray in the Spirit on all occasions and to continually pray for the Lord's people. He also tells us to be alert when it comes to praying for others. Our students are his people, and whatever the length of their stay in our classrooms, we are called to pray for them.

The command in this verse to be alert reminds us to stay present and mindful of the students in our care. In order to bring a request to God, we must first recognize the need for a request. If we keep our eyes open as we observe and communicate with our students, we can ask God to help us recognize potential needs in our midst. It's education. There is always someone in need.

What a comfort to know we can take our requests to God for any reason at any time—before, during, and after school. Praying for the students before we enter the classroom sharpens our senses to the presence of the Holy Spirit. Praying in the Spirit keeps our hearts and minds aligned with his will. Before we step foot in the door, he is waiting for us, our classrooms completely covered in his glory.

In every answered prayer, the path of provision leads directly back to the hand of the Father. Time after time I witnessed miracles in every class period. I'm sure you have too. If we stay alert, we are sure to see the evidence of God's provision all around us.

Rooted

May your practice of prayer be alert and continual—before, during, and after school.

Refreshed

Reflect on a time when you witnessed a miracle, big or small, that came as a result of your continued prayers.

21
Unmerited Grace

But God demonstrates His own love toward us, in that while we were still sinners, Christ died for us.

Romans 5:8

The tiniest phrase can stay with us forever.

I'm sure you can recall right now words spoken over your young life by a teacher, positive or negative.

My husband, Alan, was quite the challenge during his middle school years. His high energy, advanced intelligence, and quick wit made him a behavior challenge. Today he's a witty and energetic adult. I'm thoroughly convinced that being married to him equipped me for any and all behavior mishaps during my teaching career.

In seventh grade, a teacher told him he would be a high school dropout. The worst part of this story is the teacher's smile as he made the prediction for all to hear.

Thankfully, God had placed several strong male role models in my husband's life. He'd grown up without a father, and these uncles and neighbors stepped in and invested heavily in every area of his life. Hearing the stories of how they mentored him warmed my heart. Investing in another person's child—especially a challenging one—is unmerited grace in action.

Somewhere between that teacher's statement and Alan's senior year of high school, the positive influences took root. That same teacher had also moved up to the high school. He discovered that Alan was now on his senior homeroom roster.

In October he said to Alan, "Fox, when I saw your name on my roster, I went home and told my wife I was turning in my resignation. I have to say, you've grown into a very mature young man."

I am eternally grateful for the kindness and support extended to my Alan in his younger years. God stepped in with unmerited grace and paved the way for his success. From a stellar business career to a loving husband and father, God's protective hand of provision on Alan's life was clear. He tells me frequently of men who covered him in grace when he was at his most difficult to deal with—God's unmerited grace and faithful provision in action.

Grace is the cornerstone of our faith. Jesus paid the ultimate price, and we have done nothing to deserve it. "While we were still sinners, Christ died for us."

Someone took the time during my husband's young life to show him his worth. They looked past his behavior issues and invested in his potential. As educators, it doesn't take a lot of effort to see students who could use a little unmerited grace. They're right in front of us. If we're teaching middle school, the fields are plentiful. Some students are more challenging than others, but all are deserving of the same unmerited grace God extended to us. We teach in an educational culture desperate for teachers who go the extra mile. The profession is ripe with student apathy and resistance, and an outpouring of grace has the power to cover all of it.

What if we pursued student success the same way God pursues us? His search supersedes anything we've done or will do. He is unrelenting in his pursuit of us, wanting no one separated from his all-consuming love.

When we approach every student with unmerited grace, regardless of their reputation or behavior, we open the door for them to change their view of self. This life-changing grace is life-giving for us. We all know what it's like to see someone succeed, either academically or behaviorally, despite previous expectations. It's a glorious teacher moment indeed.

Our message to students can be, "I love you and think you are worthy no matter how you've acted or what you've done." Romans 5:8 in a nutshell.

Rooted

All students have promise and are worthy of unmerited grace, because this is how God sees us and them, regardless of our past and their past.

Refreshed

Reflect on a time when you extended unmerited grace and helped someone change the way they viewed their potential for the better.

22

Generosity

A generous person will prosper; whoever refreshes others will be refreshed.

Proverbs 11:25 NIV

Generosity that refreshes others. A description of the teaching profession in four words.

At the start of my career, I baked brownies for my students from time to time. It would always be a surprise. Except that time I left the surprise in the supply cabinet and we returned from break to find brownie rocks. That was a surprise.

"Wait. Mrs. Fox, you *made* these?"

Yes, I did. I'd cracked open the box, poured the brown powder into the bowl, and stirred in exactly one egg. Classroom ready in thirty-three minutes flat.

I was always in awe of how dumbfounded students were when I served up the brownies.

I'm known for a lot of things . . . being a good cook is not one of them.

I was too tired to evaluate their reactions at the time, but knowing what I know now, it makes sense. Some students don't eat regularly at home. Others don't receive much kindness. Whatever their reason, they were always grateful.

Over the years I switched from brownies to a fox-shaped cookie jar full of small, round lollipops that come in a variety of flavors. If you haven't relished one of these delicacies lately, allow me to tickle your taste buds. Each flavor offers a delicate balance between hard plastic and chemical by-products. Students *love* them.

Giving out these little goodies became the cornerstone of my teaching reputation. Word of free lollipops spreads fast.

Back to school for incoming freshmen is nothing short of terrifying. Every August I saw many frightened young people and their equally frightened parents putting on a brave face at our fall open house. I decided early on to make these latent middle schoolers and their families feel at home.

As I introduced myself and welcomed each new family to our school, I pointed the kids in the direction of the cookie jar.

"This jar holds the secret to relieving stress, and you are welcome to its contents anytime. If you ever find yourself feeling lost or stressed, please stop by my room for a lollipop."

"But what if I'm not in your class?"

"So what? Stop by anyway."

It always made me smile when they took me up on my offer. Sometimes they would bring their friends along, standing anxiously off to the side, nervous to ask me if they too could have a lollipop. My resounding "Of course!" lit their faces up like a Christmas tree. Their smiles are etched in my mind. Many of these kids were never even in my classes. I only knew them through a quick lollipop pit stop. My blessing was seeing students gasp with delight as they rooted through the jar and found their favorite flavor. A three-dollar bag of candy had given us both a moment of refreshment.

All our lives we've heard, "Giving is better than receiving." This verse in Proverbs tells us that the blessing is simultaneous. Our generosity refreshes us as we refresh others. In the original Hebrew, the word for generous is *berakah*, which also means "blessed." We all have our signature form of generosity.

You may be the teacher who stays late every day to provide extra math help or the teacher who never misses sporting events or drama performances. Teaching is generosity and sacrifice personified. You pour your time and energy into these young people, and their success is your refreshing reward. What a wonderful profession we share, in whatever capacity we choose to give. When we act with a generous spirit, the blessing goes both ways, even if it's as small and simple as offering someone a lollipop.

Rooted

Whatever our generous approach to reach across the divide and refresh their souls, we can rest in the fact that the refreshment will work both ways.

Refreshed

Reflect on an act of generosity, big or small, that refreshed both you and your students.

23

Compassion

Therefore, as God's chosen people, holy and dearly loved, clothe yourselves with compassion, kindness, humility, gentleness and patience.

Colossians 3:12 NIV

You never know what students are dealing with.

As educators, we often interpret a student's lack of interest as disrespect or apathy toward our class or curriculum.

Oh, how I wish it were only for these reasons. For most students, apathy toward the curriculum would be easier to accept than the demons staring them down.

I had the privilege of meeting an apathetic young man named Eddie in the spring of 2022. He was a senior in my drawing class. He was tall, with a quiet disposition. It didn't take long for me to realize he was struggling. Not so much with my class but with existing.

Eddie's mother had passed away several months before our semester started. He had relocated to our area to live with his grandmother the week before school began. His father was not in the picture. He suffered from extreme anxiety (not surprising) and was withdrawn as a result. He often stopped by the counselor's office during the day for some much-needed respite.

In my class, every day for Eddie was the same. I would introduce skills, pass out materials, and get everyone started, only to look over and see him with his head down, folded into his left arm, pencil in hand . . . frozen. Almost like he was trying to disappear. I was concerned. My slightly wacky and unbridled enthusiasm can normally revive even the most uninterested student. Not this time.

As I was not in the habit of passing students for doing nothing, I approached Eddie with a plan that would benefit both of us. He was so close to graduation and so far from seeing it happen. His grief was so heavy. I felt compelled to offer him a creatively compassionate alternative.

If he would draw for thirty minutes, he could spend the next twenty minutes with his counselor and the remaining thirty minutes back in class to complete the assignments for his other classes. After the shock of my proposal wore off, he gratefully agreed.

Did he create masterful works of art worthy of museum display? He did not. Did he relax enough to sit up straight and create art that helped him cope? He did. Some days he drew broken hearts surrounded by dark cloudy areas with question marks all over the paper. Some days he did his math homework. Regardless of what he did, he held up his end of the bargain.

I cannot fathom the pain of attempting to graduate so soon after my mother's funeral. It's a miracle he completed the work. His grandmother was elated when he went for a walk across that stage to receive his diploma.

Each of us is chosen and dearly loved by God. As a reflection of this love, this verse calls us to respond to others by putting on five attributes. We are to clothe ourselves with compassion, kindness, humility, gentleness, and patience. But first, compassion. The first thing others see when we approach them is our clothing. If we wear compassion like physical clothing, it is clearly visible to everyone around us. Imagine our effectiveness if we respond with compassion first in every interaction with students.

If you've been in the classroom long, you are probably recalling a similar situation. If you're new to teaching, a similar situation is on the way. Students everywhere are facing challenges beyond their years, and they desperately need to receive compassion, as well as the other attributes. Let's clothe ourselves with each of these garments that reflect God's unrelenting love for all of us and meet each student in their time of need.

Rooted

We are chosen and dearly loved by our Savior. Put on compassion, kindness, humility, gentleness, and patience. Let these be the first things your students see.

Refreshed

Reflect on a situation when you clothed yourself in compassion or another of these godly attributes and helped a student overcome a seemingly insurmountable challenge.

24
Doing Good

Let's not become discouraged in doing good, for in due time we will reap, if we do not become weary.

Galatians 6:9

I never used a traditional syllabus.

Let's face it. Nobody reads them. That first year in the classroom, I picked a lot of them up off the floor.

I decided to deliver classroom policies and procedures in an unconventional manner, one that required more student input.

I created a ten-slide policies and procedures PowerPoint syllabus. As I flipped through the slides, explaining what the students could expect from my class, everyone took notes on half a sheet of scrap construction paper. A cost-effective and simple approach to getting rid of those neon shades of yellow, green, and pink leftovers. Because the presentation was short and they wrote everything down, it stuck.

The presentation was full of feedback from past students, comments taken from the course evaluation at the end of the previous semester. Every slide contained a few comments, which served to lighten the expectation anxiety. I could tell them all day long what to expect in my class and it wouldn't resonate. When they heard it from their peers, it carried more weight.

At semester's end I was both nervous and excited to read those forms. Students at the high school level have a weak filter, and they never fail to give it to you straight.

I was about to receive my performance evaluation from the only earthly source that mattered.

One semester I had a senior in my painting class who came to school only half the time. He had a surly attitude and hardly ever did his work. When he did attempt something, it usually ended up unfinished. No matter what I did, from endless encouraging conversations, behavior strategies, and parental involvement, he was on the verge of dropping out.

The situation left me weary and discouraged.

Incredibly, he managed to show up at the end of the semester to take the final exam and fill out his course evaluation. I'm not gonna lie—I couldn't wait to read his feedback.

In response to the question about how to be successful in my class, he wrote this: "Do your work. Mrs. Fox expects 100% all day every day. Not because she's mean. Because she truly cares about all of us. Even my sorry ass." It is one of the few comments with a permanent place in the yearly syllabus presentation.

God's command is for us to do good for our students without growing weary. It says nothing about the time frame or the results. The reaping in due time is God's job. The not-becoming-weary part is ours. Notice that the verse says, "not become weary." This tells me we don't start out weary. We start fresh and slowly (or quickly) work ourselves to weary, fretting over why the good isn't producing results in our due time.

What if all we need is a shift in our focus? When Paul says we will reap in due time, maybe the reaping is our peace of mind knowing that God is in control.

Education is results driven. What if we forget the results and remain laser-focused on the act of doing good? In Greek, the word "good" is translated as *kalos*. Its definitions are "honorable," "honest," "commendable," and "excellent." What if we poured out honorable, honest, commendable, and excellent good on every student and every circumstance and left it to God to do the rest?

After graduation I learned that my apathetic student had voluntarily and successfully completed an intense substance-abuse treatment program. I had nearly worn myself to a frazzle thinking he hated my class, that I had failed to reach him. Turns out he was just trying to hang on the entire time.

Rooted

Let's serve our students as we commit ourselves to doing good without growing weary. We can be confident that God will take care of the rest.

Refreshed

Reflect on a time when the demands of teaching threatened your stamina, and God strengthened your perseverance.

25
Ever-Present

God is our refuge and strength,
an ever-present help in trouble.
Therefore we will not fear, though the earth give way
and the mountains fall into the heart of the sea,
though its waters roar and foam
and the mountains quake with their surging.

Psalm 46:1–3 NIV

I had a really nice teacher's desk, next to a giant row of windows overlooking a beautiful courtyard.

I hardly ever sat there.

With at least one student absent daily, I preferred to sit in one of the vacant student seats.

"Do you mind if I sit here?"

At the beginning of the semester, I got more than a few raised eyebrows.

As I pulled out the chair, I noticed the smiles and the shifting as students sat up straighter. My paperwork consumed half the table, but nobody seemed to mind. The only thing missing was my ice-cold cup of coffee (still currently MIA—who can relate?). It's counterintuitive to think that teenagers would actually *want* the teacher sitting at their table, but they do.

Where we stand, sit, and talk with students speaks volumes. In teaching programs, they call this classroom-management strategy "proximity." In short, it says we should stay close to students physically to curb potential behavior issues. I preferred to view it as a comfort strategy, telling my students (without telling them) I'm close by and ready to help in a moment of need. Whether it improves behavior or assures students of their safety, it's effective.

A student told me once that she couldn't wait to get back to the safety of my classroom. She knew that inside those four walls she felt safe.

Her father had taken his life when she was a freshman—during my first year teaching and her first year in high school. No one needed safety more than she did. Inexperienced as I was, I rested in God's refuge as I helped her navigate this tragic event. I recall constantly pleading for his wisdom and direction. He not only provided both wisdom and direction, but he also taught me how to minister amid grief I had never experienced myself. It was a valuable lesson in meeting someone in their pain with nothing more than my quiet presence.

Moving forward from this horrifying event, I asked God for insight into all avenues to create a safe space for students. How do we assure them that we are ever present? Not just because we are physically in the classroom but are actively at the ready to ensure their safety and success. I know it sounds simple, but where we place ourselves among our students sends a message mirroring God's commitment to us. *If anything happens, I'm right here with you.*

It's comforting to know that help is close by just in case we need it. If we know Jesus as our personal Savior, we are confident that the maker of the universe lives inside our hearts, providing a sense of peace and safety like no other. This verse tells us he is an "ever-present" help in times of trouble—and that when that trouble comes, it can be devastating. The trouble described in verses two and three is frightening on a whole other level.

In our classrooms and personal lives, trouble is destined to make an appearance. It's a given. Fortunately, God's presence is also a given. Another definition of *ever present* is "constantly or continuously there." We need not go searching for help from outside sources. Anything outside of God's wisdom and guidance can potentially fail us (or even harm us) at any moment. God is our only guaranteed perfect source of help. He cannot fail us, he is always present, and he is waiting to come to our aid. All we have to do is ask.

Rooted

Take comfort that God positions himself in our hearts as an ever-present help. He is at the ready as our continuous source of safety and strength.

Refreshed

Reflect on occasions when God has reminded you of his ever-present location in your heart and your life.

26
No Excuses

Therefore, since we also have such a great cloud of witnesses surrounding us, let's rid ourselves of every obstacle and the sin which so easily entangles us, and let's run with endurance the race that is set before us.

Hebrews 12:1

"Everybody has something."

My go-to response to any excuse for not getting the job done. Any job.

Excuses come in all shapes and sizes, and some of them are lame.

"I didn't have time to finish."

"I wish I had more time to finish, but . . . [insert lame excuse]."

Time is the currency of life. It's the one thing that levels the playing field—an equal portion for every person. Twenty-four fresh, new hours each day, provided we wake up and breathe through all twenty-four hours. Waking up is the ultimate gift.

Teaching advanced art and portfolio prep courses is similar to coaching a cross-country team. The race is consistently long and steady. The entire school year is a marathon of art-making, interspersed with hard deadlines, and little room for missing or incomplete work.

Deadlines being what they are, I dedicated specific discussions to helping students learn how to manage time effectively. We talked about the blessings of freedom, mobility, opportunity, and placement. When broken down into segments and examined objectively, it was as if they were seeing the gift of their lives for the first time. Once students grasped the concept of this gift, the lame excuses dwindled into nonexistence.

There's nothing like a real-life threat to the gift to send a time-management message over the goal line.

It's at this point that I need to tell you about Shelby.

Shelby was one of my advanced students, bright-eyed and filled with raw God-given talent. In her sophomore year, after months of repeated illness, she received a diagnosis of pre-B-cell acute lymphoblastic leukemia. As horrifying as the news was, Shelby's parents armored up for the battle with Jesus in command. A fortress of strength and positive energy. They committed to fortify Shelby with the Lord's strength to enable her to run this daunting race to remission with steadfast dignity.

This family allowed no excuses. In her entire two-year raging war against childhood cancer, she remained in school—albeit homebound most of the time. I had the privilege of working with her at home. On one occasion, her father carried her downstairs and sat her at the kitchen table for our lesson. She was too weak to walk. I never heard one excuse.

Shelby won her final battle against cancer the summer before her senior year. What a blessing it was to see her back in school as part of my AP portfolio class. A living reminder of running the race with endurance. She and her parents could have easily given in to fear and self-pity if her focus misplaced on things that ensnare and entangle.

She and her family chose to focus on the positive, clinging to the Lord and his healing strength for every challenge along the way. And what a cloud of witnesses they had, from fellow patients to classmates to friends and family all over the country. Shelby and her family had the opportunity to run their race publicly, glorifying God and inspiring people at every turn.

Shelby's story became a permanent fixture in my time-management discussions with future classes. Watching her fulfill her responsibilities during her illness gave me a beautiful context to share with students. I shared her journey frequently, even after she graduated and remained in remission, living out her beautiful best life in her mid-twenties.

Each one of us is running a race. For the classroom marathon, the obstacle of misplaced focus has no place in our pace. Just as we want accountability for our students, God wants accountability for us. When we take our eyes off Jesus, the heavy burdens of fear, doubt, or worry threaten to slow us down. When we look to the Lord for every ounce of strength and energy to run this race called life, God is in the center of our situation. He promises to help us rid our lives of anything that is holding us back. Teaching is a marathon, and our endurance is guaranteed when we focus on the good, making no excuses along the way.

Rooted

What a blessing to run this race called teaching, with our wonderful students—a cloud of witnesses chosen by the Lord.

Refreshed

Reflect on a time when you saw a student run a difficult race filled with strength and endurance, completely free of excuses.

27
Impartial

But the wisdom from above is first pure, then peace-loving, gentle, reasonable, full of mercy and good fruits, impartial, free of hypocrisy.

James 3:17

My initial reaction as I read this verse was, "Wow, God is so good."

As I think about how this applies to the classroom, I am struck by the word "impartial."

Our students span a wide range of abilities and scheduling scenarios. We art teachers, and other enhancement teachers, often think certain students are *dumped* into our classes.

On the contrary, with God's schedule, there is no dumping. The students on our rosters are perfectly positioned for the appointed time.

I know what you're thinking. And yes, even the most difficult students.

As we look over the roster, how do we view these students? Are we so anxious to meet the "creative and talented" few—imagining their wins in the competition arena—that we overlook the other twenty-nine students? Do we approach everyone on our roster with equal time and energy? For most students, the art-room win will never be prizeworthy.

I had a young lady enter my beginner drawing class in the spring of her senior year. She was "dumped" there at the last minute—evidently accounting had no more seats open. Her younger sister was in my advanced drawing class, and her natural artistic talent cast a large and looming shadow over her older sister.

She entered my classroom with hesitation and a declaration. "I'm just warning you—I'm nothing like my sister. I'm *not* artistic."

"You're not supposed to be. You're here to learn to draw, and when this class is over, you will be amazed at how artistic you are."

We spent the entire semester building our drawing skills, as a group, with every student receiving the same level of input and assistance. Our last unit was colored pencil, a difficult art medium that requires a lot of patience and hard work.

When I close my eyes, I can still picture it.

A scoop of vanilla ice cream in a waffle cone, turned over and beginning to melt. Multicolored candy pieces sliding off the ice cream onto the table. The background was a vibrant turquoise blue. A skillful, spectacular drawing indeed.

"I can't believe I drew this. You were right—I'm amazed."

When we approach every student in the room with equal expectations, God's loving impartiality is evident. Impartiality that encourages and prepares students to succeed before they ever draw their first line, solve their first math problem, write their first sentence, or debate their first topic.

Impartiality is challenging, especially when raw talent is dominant. It's tempting to gravitate to the talented students, primed and ready to create artwork teachers only dream of. The teacher payoff can be anything from merit pay to blue ribbons to national recognition. Who among us doesn't love sweeping the awards at a nationwide competition? Can you say "Ego boost"? I know I can. The hard reality is actually humbling. The talented students are the people who need us the least. Sure, watching them think, plan, and create is fun, and they soak up every skill we teach them like a kitchen sponge.

God sees all of us as chosen and appointed for a purpose. He sees our students in the same light. We convey this message when we approach every student equally. Students feel seen, valued, and worthy regardless of their level of raw talent. The student work that stems from this feeling of value is nothing short of amazing.

The ego tells us to focus on the raw talent for the most teacher gain. God says to focus on each student with equal energy and lofty expectation. This focus is God's wisdom from above. It is a wisdom that is pure, peace-loving, gentle, reasonable, full of mercy and good fruits, *impartial*, and free of hypocrisy. The perfect combination to reach our students for their full potential.

Rooted

Approach every student as God approaches us, impartially and free of hypocrisy. He desires all of us to grow to our full potential.

Refreshed

Reflect on a time when you witnessed a student exceed expectations as a result of your impartial approach.

28
Respect and Compassion

You, Lord, will not withhold Your compassion from me; Your mercy and Your truth will continually watch over me.

Psalm 40:11

"Mrs. Fox, this class feels different. It's like we're a family."

"That's because we are. We will never be together in this place with these same people ever again. We have one goal—fabulousness. Everything that prevents us from achieving this goal has no place in this classroom."

Clearly defined purpose resonates. As the semester unfolded, I never heard, "Why are we doing this? Is this for a grade?" While grades are important, the grade was not the endgame. Fabulousness was the endgame.

Compassion and mercy were intricately woven into our classroom purpose. Over the course of the semester, each person became acutely aware of how they could contribute to the success of their classmates. It was always heartwarming to see the classroom community take shape.

The first two rules in my classroom were "Respect the teacher" and "Respect each other." Respect and compassion go hand in hand. Just as God does not withhold compassion from me, I wanted compassion to be free-flowing in my classroom. From me to the students and from student to student. A sea of kindness washing over everyone, my vision of the perfect classroom.

A few years ago, we had the privilege of knowing Connor as part of our beginner drawing family. Connor was born with autism, and emotional anxiety was a dominant part of his daily life. When he became agitated, I would kneel beside his table and talk with him quietly until he regained his peace. When the emotions became overwhelming, we adjourned to the hallway for a serene moment to regroup.

The gift of the innate ability to control my emotions was completely lost on me until I began teaching. We are surrounded by students struggling with emotional issues, some of which they are unable to control. In some cases they have no one to show them how to get through it. Modeling the compassion and mercy seen in Psalm 40:11 provides all our students with a framework for how to recognize and respond not only to their own emotional needs, but also to the needs of others.

One day as Connor was working on his drawing, frustration got the better of him, and he erupted into a vocal outburst. Before I could get to him, a young man sitting two tables over hurried and knelt next to Connor. Speaking softly, he said, "I'm right here, Connor. It's gonna be okay, buddy. Tell me how I can help."

Every other student in the room continued working without pause. They knew of Connor's struggles. The young man who went to his aid had struggles of his own. He battled a constant, uncontrollable tremor in both hands. As he spoke words of support to Connor, the other students at the table joined in, quietly reassuring their friend that all was well.

Stressors in the classroom can bring us to the breaking point. I'm quite sure several are rolling through your mind as you read this sentence. In the face of these stressors, it's important to remember our ability to handle them. What a blessing to consciously maintain our composure with something as simple as a deep breath. We are privileged to work through this blessing as we come alongside students who struggle to cope with their emotions. Our compassion and mercy, in every word and deed, is an outpouring of God's love in the midst of a stressful moment.

Continually watching over these souls with compassion and mercy is paramount to their understanding rule two—respect each other. How will they learn the value of caring for those around them unless we demonstrate compassion and mercy in our classrooms? What a gift it is to share the love of Christ with our students, caring for them as Christ cares for us. The atmosphere in our classes overflowing with students who continually watch over one another.

Watching Connor be calmed by the compassion of another student while the class rallied around him made my heart full.

Rooted

When we continually flood our classroom with God's overflowing compassion and mercy, the result is a roomful of students who continually watch over one another.

Refreshed

Reflect on a situation when students in your classroom came to the unsolicited aid of a fellow learner in their time of need.

29

Lifting Each Other Up

Two are better than one because they have a good return for their labor; for if either of them falls, the one will lift up his companion. But woe to the one who falls when there is not another to lift him up!

Ecclesiastes 4:9–10

We've been hijacked.

Technology is in control, especially at the middle and high school levels. Everyone in the building is carrying or wearing a device of some sort.

Administering tests in a cheat-free zone is a real challenge. Back in my day, they checked us for notes written on our forearms and ankles. Nowadays it's all about the tech.

Kids have a difficult time giving up their phones for any reason. The addiction is real. Getting the entire class to relinquish their phones is quite the endeavor.

Back in the early days of my career, I was in desperate need of a solution for "cell phone separation anxiety," especially on test days. A popular TV show led me to an idea. I would create a runway-style fashion show exclusively for cellular devices. As corny as this is about to sound, you gotta try it. It works.

On test days, these words were written on the board in big flowery letters: "Fox's Fabulous Phone Fashion Show!" A row of arrows pointed downward toward the board's metal ledge.

Students powered down their phones, turned them with the case side facing out, and wrote their names above them. All the different phone cases, pop sockets, and credit card holders were fun to see. It honestly looked like a fashion show on the otherwise boring whiteboard.

"These phones say something about each of us. Look at all the beautiful and interesting cases. We even have phones with no case at all for those of us living on the edge. When we separate ourselves from distraction, we open the door for clarity and focus, and success is easier to achieve. More importantly, when we are quiet and focused, we offer the person next to us a chance to succeed."

No one touched the phones until everyone was finished with the test. Not even me.

In the early days of Fox's Fabulous Phone Fashion Show, the kids were nervous. "Are we in trouble?" "Are you going to take my phone?"

Once they understood the *why* behind the exercise, the anxiety subsided. The community goal was clear: success for everyone, with everyone playing an important role. No one was singled out and no one was left out. Not only were they being included, but they were sacrificing their own needs for the needs of their classmates. When the message was delivered with a sense of value and purpose, nobody wanted to be left out. Even if it meant giving up that precious cell phone for an hour.

In our classrooms, God has provided a ready-made "family." People we can receive support from and offer support to. A good return for our daily labor. Helping someone else warms both the heart and soul. It's God's natural design that we feel good when we help others. Students are no different. They are not nearly as self-centered as the world would like us to believe.

For many young people, loneliness is where they live. Our classrooms harbor the potential to destroy student isolation, to be a safe space for belonging and support. A place where we cultivate an atmosphere of helping one another succeed, of lifting one another up. A small sacrifice (no phone) during a test is no longer seen as personal deprivation, but a chance to help someone else do well. Our students begin to view life as a group effort.

The admonition is clear. Woe to the person in isolation who has no one to lift him up. God surrounds us with people in every season and situation. Each person is in our presence for a reason. What a gift. Thirty-plus young people to show God's love to as we support, work alongside, and lift one another up.

Rooted

How blessed we are to demonstrate the love of God as we cultivate in our students an attitude of helping one another!

Refreshed

Reflect on a scenario when you saw students sacrifice something for the success of their classmates.

30
Fear Is a Liar

Then David said to his son Solomon, "Be strong and courageous, and act; do not fear nor be dismayed, for the Lord God, my God, is with you. He will not fail you nor forsake you until all the work for the service of the house of the Lord is finished."

1 Chronicles 28:20

Satan's advances are a real thing, and fear is his primary weapon. Its grip is tight and suffocating. So how do we escape it?

I have a dear friend who loves me with unrelenting grace. She follows the Lord closely, and her ears and heart are open any time I need to talk. Friends like these are precious and few. When I made the life-changing decision to leave the classroom, she served as a stabilizing force, reminding me of God's faithfulness during my transition season.

One day we were talking about the thoughts that wrecked our courage. At that time I had a long list. I was fresh out of the classroom, flailing around like a fish out of water. She listened quietly as I described every possible scenario that stoked the flames in my mind. I was convinced that outside of teaching, my life was completely without purpose.

When I was finished, she looked at me calmly and said, "Well . . . whenever my mind begins to carry me into scary places, I ask myself a simple question. Is this *true*?"

There it was. No judgment. Just a guiding question of introspection. And once I went through my list of impending doomsday disasters with this simple question in mind, the answer was, "Well, even if the worst happens (and it very likely won't), do I believe that God can handle the worst?"

The fact of the matter is, whatever our fears of the future are, none of us have a clue what will occur after this moment in time. Right now I'm typing and still wondering if anyone will ever read this book. Right now you're reading, and your mind is most likely battling at least one fear of the unknown. Now is the only thing we can be sure of. We both know that God is with us and he can handle it. His Word assures us that he is with us, and he's not going anywhere until the work is finished.

I was convinced my life had no purpose outside of teaching. Something tells me there may be purpose in these pages. I just had to stop residing in fear, trust God, and act.

Almost two years ago, God began to call me to write this book, I was petrified at first, but finally I asked him what he wanted me to write; and as he revealed it, I began to type. A few months ago I thought I was finished—and then God sent me a devotional author coach who changed the course of my work. She told me this book had promise but that a multitude of revisions were still needed.

As she spoke these words on our very first Zoom call, the fear consumed me all over again.

After the call my mind was racing. *I thought I was finished! I can't do this! I'm not an author! Who do I think I am?*

I dialed up my friend, unleashed my chaotic thoughts, and waited for the wisdom. Her response was life giving. "Tiff, listen to yourself. Seriously? Is this *true*? Hasn't God already brought you this far? This author coach says your work has promise. Maybe God sent her because he knew that without her, the project would not meet his guidelines."

Preach it, dear friend.

Sitting with fear takes time and energy. Fear subsides and work is accomplished when we sit with God and move forward in his calling. David is commanding Solomon in this verse to build the temple free of fear, and tells him that as he builds it according to God's guidelines, God will not fail him or forsake him. These words are just as true for us. We can march into our classrooms every day, filled with God's calling and purpose, confident that he is with us every step of the way.

God will provide every aspect of wisdom and strength necessary as you complete the work in your classroom. Remember, God's character is unchanging, and fear is not welcome in this place.

Rooted

God has equipped you for whatever and whoever comes next. Breathe into this truth. If he has planned it, you can handle it.

Refreshed

Reflect on a time when you released your fears, trusted God, and leaned into his calling.

31
The Rudder

Look at the ships too: though they are so large and are driven by strong winds, they are nevertheless directed by a very small rudder wherever the inclination of the pilot determines. So also the tongue is a small part of the body, and yet it boasts of great things.

James 3:4–5

The early years of teaching are often filled with fear that is nothing short of irrational.

I spent my first two years in the classroom with a permanent knot in my stomach. As I gained confidence in one area, I moved on to allow the next fear to wreck my system.

I knew better.

I had spent the better part of ten years praying for my own classroom. Now it was a reality. Amazing students sitting in front of me daily, and together we were building a classroom community where everyone could succeed. God's faithfulness was never more evident than now.

Instead of resting in his faithfulness and my reality, what did I do? I allowed the most ridiculous circumstances to consume me with fear. I fantasized about every little thing that could possibly go wrong. On occasion this approach sent me spiraling into the abyss of the ridiculous.

One morning I was preparing to lecture via a PowerPoint presentation. As the students arrived and settled in, I couldn't locate the remote control for the projector. My fear gained momentum as I paced around the room, searching feverishly and trying to remain calm.

In my head a voice was sounding the alarm. *Someone took it! Now what?! They're making a fool out of you and there's nothing you can do about it!* (Never mind the fact that I could advance the slides manually.)

As I circled the room once again, I was close to tears. The lights were out, the kids were all sitting quietly with their notes, and there I was pacing back and forth like a crazy woman.

My thoughts raged faster. *Listen, people, the jig is up! When I find out who took my remote, it's gonna be on!*

"Mrs. Fox, are you looking for the remote? It's right here."

I turned to see a young man reaching his hand toward me, holding my remote. He hadn't taken it. He was sitting by the back counter, and that's where he found it—right where I'd left it the day before. No shenanigans. No thievery. Just me not putting it back in my desk, where it belonged.

Not only did I feel like an idiot, I felt ashamed that I had assumed the worst. The rudder of fear had hijacked the ship, negating everything I knew to be true of my students. They had never given me cause to think they would steal anything, much less my remote. I had almost given in to Satan's false accusations.

The Enemy knows the power of a God-fearing teacher. He is intent on destroying our classroom rapport, and he will use anything in the room to do it—even a tiny remote control. If he can convince us of their wrongdoing, then maybe we will crack and falsely accuse them. Thank goodness the rudder of ridiculousness only screamed in my head. Something as simple as a misplaced remote had threatened to ruin our classroom community.

The Enemy would love nothing more than to cause us to say something unkind that would permanently fracture the trust of our students. The rudder of fear influencing the rudder of the tongue, sending the ship of our classroom community off course. Fear and anxiety will never cease to exist, but our hope is in Christ to remind us what is true. We can reflect on his goodness, and he will keep us grounded in reality instead of caving into irrational fear and anxious thoughts.

Rooted

Focusing on God shifts the rudder. We can focus on fear and draw the energy to steer toward the irrational, or we can focus on God and steer toward his truth.

Refreshed

Reflect on a situation when you almost caved to the fear, but God swept in with his fear-busting support and reminded you of what is true.

32
Take It to God First

Then Hezekiah took the letter from the hand of the messengers and read it, and he went up to the house of the Lord and spread it out before the Lord. Hezekiah prayed before the Lord and said, "Lord, God of Israel, enthroned above the cherubim, You are the God, You alone, of all the kingdoms of the earth. You have made heaven and earth. Incline Your ear, Lord, and hear; open Your eyes, Lord, and see; and listen to the words of Sennacherib, which he has sent to taunt the living God."

2 Kings 19:14–16

I don't know what you're facing. What you walk into each day—stomach churning, heart pounding.

In all your worldly physical strength, it just never seems like enough.

Because it isn't.

Sometimes God brings us to desperate places to remind us who he is.

When things become too much, we can take a page from Hezekiah's playbook. Go to the Lord, spread the letter before him, and give him the report.

Allow me to suggest some common lies the Enemy sends our way.

"These kids are out of control."

"Nobody cares."

"I can't do this."

Whatever you're saying about your current situation, God is acutely aware of the details and every person involved. He hears your report and has a solution, even if you can't see it.

During the pandemic lockdown, my limited knowledge of technology was crushing my will to teach. "I can't do this" was my daily mantra. Everything I knew about teaching had dissolved into thin air. With no students physically in the room, every classroom strategy and motivational technique was utterly useless. The game had a new playbook, and it was written in hieroglyphics.

Shortly after lockdown began, a teacher in a Facebook group inquired about online colored-pencil classes for art educators. Another teacher commented, "Let's ask Tiffany Fox—she's the colored-pencil expert."

I offered to teach colored-pencil techniques online to art teachers. As the classes approached, the voice of the Adversary grew increasingly louder. I heard everything from "You can't figure this out" to "Nobody's going to sign up" to "You're irrelevant." With no formal experience teaching online, I had to start from scratch. Instead of imploding (which seemed like the best idea at times), I pulled that page from Hezekiah's playbook and I spread it all out before the Lord.

"Lord, I have no idea what is required to teach live classes online. What I do know is that people do this every day. Just because I don't know how right now doesn't mean I can't learn. You have equipped me with the smarts, the ability, and the time. Please provide wise people who are capable of helping me get this project off the ground."

And that's exactly what he did. That summer I taught colored-pencil techniques and teaching strategies to more than three hundred teachers—online. He brought me an unexpected blessing in a knowledgeable young lady to act as my technical adviser. Her knowledge and assistance allowed me to focus on the teaching and not the technology. I finished that summer teaching just shy of thirty online workshops. My technical adviser has since created a permanent online site with more than eleven hundred educators enrolled in coursework. When I click on the home page, I am still in awe of my feelings of inadequacy and how God moved and provided in that season.

When the voices get loud, we need to take every fear-filled problem to the Lord first. We can spread the letter in front of him and tell him about our fears. Tell him what the world is saying and how frightened we are. Hezekiah did not pass Go and he didn't collect any money first. He went straight to the Lord. What a beautiful picture of trust.

Rooted

I don't know what you're facing or what the voice of the Enemy is saying. What I do know is this: God is present in your situation. Whatever it is, take it to him first.

Refreshed

Reflect on a time when you bypassed the voice of the Enemy and fear and took your concerns straight to the Lord, spread them before him, and told him all about them.

33
Fixed

Let your eyes look directly ahead and let your gaze be fixed straight in front of you. Watch the path of your feet, and all your ways will be established.

Proverbs 4:25–26

Today's teaching climate can cause even the most seasoned educator to feel inadequate.

With the advent of social media, we face an onslaught of apparent success in thousands of classrooms around the world. If we do not remain fixed on the success of our own students, watching the path of our own feet, comparison can threaten our confidence and destroy our peace.

My best advice? Stop looking around. Your path is yours and no one else's. Everything about your situation is unique and ordained specifically for you and your students. All these glitzy video clips and pro tips, while created by well-intended teachers, are not your experience. They belong to someone else.

This passage tells us to fix our eyes directly on God, without deviation, changing direction, or stopping. Verse 26 tells us to watch "the path of your feet." A path is literally a way that is formed by continual treading. I often wonder about the pathways I create with continual treading—especially in my mind.

The Enemy uses the smoke and mirrors of another teacher's social media feed to shake our resolve. Glitzy posts are a snapshot devoid of context. We know nothing beyond the confines of the post. Why, then, do we see this teacher as doing a better job than we are? The shifting sand of social media is a dangerous place to establish one's worth.

God is giving us two specific directives: fix our gaze and watch where we walk (or how we think). We have a wealth of blessings in our own classrooms, free of the filters and trending audio. God's children are in our rooms for a divine appointment. We all have something to learn from their time in our room.

Every day at the start of class, I stood and fixed my gaze on my students. "Thank you for getting up early and coming to school. I missed you, and I am so glad you're here." It's a little awkward the first few times. Based on their expressions, I'm fairly sure they do not get this same greeting in other classes. After a week or so, it's pretty cool to see them sitting patiently at the start of class, expectantly waiting for the welcome.

It can be tempting to imagine how perfect someone else's life is. The lie goes something like this: If we only had their students, their huge classroom space, and their art budget, things would be so much better.

The reality is, students are people, and people are flawed no matter their socioeconomic status. Every subsection of the population has its own set of challenges. Wishing we taught different students is futile. If the Enemy can keep us wishing for another situation, he succeeds in stealing our focus (and joy) from the path in front of us. Let's not waste time wishing for another set of students, another classroom, or a bigger budget. Instead, let's fix our eyes on our own students and meet their needs.

When we fix our eyes on God, comparison to others seems ridiculous. If we see something cool happening in another classroom online, but our eyes are firmly fixed on God and our own experience, these highlighted moments act as inspiration and not comparison. Those seemingly perfect classrooms go from places of envy to spaces of inspiration.

If we truly believe that God has covered our classrooms with provision and purpose, it's easy to focus on the path ahead, because we know who's in control. God has gifted us with specific abilities, students, our current classroom space (no matter how small), and our classroom budget (no matter how small). Staying in the present space and seeking God's guidance leads us to new insights, reasons to be thankful, and fresh ideas—this is God in action, establishing all our ways.

Rooted

Regardless of what we see on our device, God has specifically designed our current classroom situations. Let's fix our eyes on serving our students and looking straight ahead, through our own classroom door.

Refreshed

Reflect on a time when you fixed your eyes straight ahead, keeping your sights on God and his current plan and season for your life, instead of someone else's, no matter how good their life might seem.

34
Safety and Rejoicing

The Lord your God is in your midst,
A victorious warrior.
He will rejoice over you with joy,
He will be quiet in His love,
He will rejoice over you with shouts of joy.

Zephaniah 3:17

"Mrs. Fox, can I stay here all day?"

You're smiling right now because you've heard this question too. I know—it's fun in the art room, and yes, kids generally love being there.

But what if you teach math? (If you teach math and your kids wanna stay all day, *you* need to write a book!)

Some classroom environments are magnetic—students are drawn to them even if they don't take the class. These classrooms aren't just places to create art or solve equations. Students feel safe in these places. We had a calculus teacher at our school whose room was packed before and after school and during lunch. If you didn't get there early, you were sitting on the floor. This teacher exuded kindness and grace. His room was steeped in community. I never came right out and asked, but I'm willing to bet this person is a Jesus follower. A selfless vibe of service was evident in all aspects of his teaching style.

He always stood in the hallway outside his classroom door, greeting students with an enthusiastic welcome as they approached. Their faces lit up every time (and these kids were going to calculus). I knew a great strategy when I saw one, so I followed suit. Between classes I would stand outside my door and call out to students as they approached. "Are you ready to be fabulous? Get in here—quick!" They looked at me like I was nuts, their steps a little quicker, faces full of smiles. They could be sure of one thing. The next ninety minutes would be filled with victorious shouts of joy.

If your birthday fell within our eighteen-week semester, you were in for a treat. I performed an overexaggerated Broadway-style a cappella version of the "Happy Birthday" song, complete with dance moves and a big "Star-Spangled Banner"–style finish. Talk about hilarious. It acquired such a reputation that as soon as the semester began, students would come up and say, "My birthday is this semester! Are you going to sing to me?"

In my case, the creator of heaven and earth was in room 357 every day for thirteen years. I told my students that this room was where the joy resided. "Regardless of how you express your rejoicing, declare victory for everyone to hear."

So why do students gravitate to certain classroom environments? Classrooms covered in a quiet love, welcoming every student with rejoicing, are magnetic. This is not just art class or math class. It's an opportunity to safely be yourself as you contribute to a unique community. A chance to be the best version of you without fear of judgment. As we serve students with a quiet love that reflects God's service, a feeling of security is the natural outcome. People who feel safe naturally want to stay around for more safety. Safety leads to rejoicing, both for us and for our students.

The Lord is in our midst. As teachers, how can we experience anything but a safe sense of rejoicing when God is at the top of our roster? The wording is not, "The Lord your God is watching from a distance." He is in our midst. Leading with a secure and quiet love that never leaves the room, his attendance is perfect. I picture his name on the roster written as "Alpha"—the beginning of every soul in the room. One more reason for us to rejoice.

Imagine a room where we lead with a quiet love, claim victory over every student, and establish a safe space as we rejoice over students with shouts of joy. Our students need all these components to succeed. Some students respond to a quiet approach, and others relish in the exuberant rejoicing. As we teach and lead with both strategies, we can rejoice knowing that our safe spaces are covered in his victorious love, every day.

Rooted

The Lord is in our midst. Here in our classrooms, basking in the joy along with us as we shout the victory for all to hear.

Refreshed

Reflect on a fellow teacher whose classroom environment was steeped in a spirit of welcome, love, and rejoicing. A classroom students never wanted to leave.

35
Rejoicing and Gentle

Rejoice in the Lord always; again I will say, rejoice! Let your gentle spirit be known to all people. The Lord is near.

Philippians 4:4–5

Describe your classroom-management style in one word. What word would your students use?

We spend an exhaustive amount of time trying to modify student behavior.

Maybe it's not their behavior that needs to be modified.

Maybe it's ours.

I've read these two verses on countless occasions. Today I read the words "rejoice" and "gentle" in light of my role as an educator.

To rejoice means to "experience gladness."[3] Here's the thing about joy. Joy is not a circumstantial good feeling. Joy is happiness that transcends circumstances. A permanent state of being based on who God is, not what is happening around us.

When are we supposed to rejoice? Always. Not just when life is good. This is the "for better or worse" component of joy.

When we abide in a state of joy, our entire mood is tempered in the face of controversy. For example, there will be occasions when a gentle spirit toward a

---

3. "*Merriam-Webster Collegiate*," "rejoice," accessed September 2, 2025, https://unabridged.merriam-webster.com/unabridged/rejoice.

team teacher is much more challenging than anything we face with students. (Yikes. That's another devotion entirely.)

Verse five tells us we are to let "all people" know of our gentle spirit. Not only a gentleness toward our students, but toward our coworkers as well.

I define the word *gentle* another way too: "to be patient when annoyed." (Insert photo of any classroom teacher next to definition of "gentle.")

Some annoyances are temporary and others last the entire year. I'm sure you have several annoying moments returning to your mind at this very moment.

Here are a few of my personal favorites:

- In the middle of a lecture, someone says, "When is this going to be over?"
- The office calls at the beginning of critique—early dismissal for the student who just set up to present their work.
- Returning from a day off to find the work left for the students incomplete and a sink full of crusty paint brushes.
- Yet another UFC-style fight in the hallway just as we begin our drawing demonstration.
- Fire drill in the middle of a quiz.

"Mrs. Fox, why don't you ever get mad and yell?"

"Would that change anything?"

Well, possibly. But not for the better.

It sounds strange, but in a tense moment I would take a deep breath and rejoice (in my head, of course) in having students to be aggravated with in the first place. I tried my best to keep my focus on the gift of their youthful presence, regardless of their actions.

The classroom is filled with triggers that threaten our gentleness. Unfortunately, anger never fails to open the door for thoughtless and damaging words. We choose whether or not to walk through. Students are always watching and listening, whether we realize it or not. We teach a valuable life skill every time we respond in a moment of frustration.

American essayist James Baldwin said it best: "Children have never been very good at listening to their elders, but they have never failed to imitate them. They must, they have no other models."[4]

Your struggles are not the same as mine or anyone else's. The good news is, we serve a God who is faithful to provide exactly what we lack in every tense moment. All we have to do is ask. Whatever our challenges are, we can rejoice knowing he is faithful to fill us to capacity with a spirit of rejoicing. He promises to help keep us gentle in all circumstances.

Rooted

Managing our responses in a tense moment is no easy task. If we allow him, God promises us a safe place to remain—joyful and gentle.

Refreshed

Reflect on a time when your focus on God helped you remain joyful and gentle during a tense classroom moment.

4. James Baldwin, *Nobody Knows My Name* (Vintage, 1992), 61–62.

36
Filled

For He has satisfied the thirsty soul,
And He has filled the hungry soul with what is good.
Psalm 107:9

As I sit here asking God what to type next, I'm listening to a song from 2007 by the group Need to Breathe, titled, "Washed by the Water."

It's perfectly timed for my current season, and yet it reminds me of days gone by.

After all this time, I can still see the two-lane road in my mind, twisting through the countryside as it carried me from my home in Mooresville to the University of North Carolina at Charlotte.

A little backstory is in order. In 2007 my one-way commute to college was forty minutes. I was back in school at the age of forty, new to the area, managing a family with a husband who traveled for work, and hoping to graduate the following year. It was more than a little nerve-racking at times. To calm my nerves, I listened to uplifting Christian music during the drive.

That forty minutes in the car was my time to cry out to God. The radio offered me a flood of Christian music to remind me how big God is and how much he loves me.

Our pastor had challenged us recently to reflect on what we allowed into our headspace—specifically, what we listened to. He framed it as the "fuel" that fills our tank. I had never really thought about it before, but as I considered my "fuel," some of it was a little low on octane. If I'm being honest, most of it was worthless.

It's at our most vulnerable points that Satan sees the greatest chance for victory. Life-giving fortification is necessary if we wish to stay the course, to advance in God's plan and purpose for our lives. In 2007 I was in a tenuous headspace, and this music filled my hungry and thirsty soul. As God's Word satisfied my anxious soul, I saw hope for the days ahead—mostly hope for employment.

That was eighteen years ago. I'm smiling again because at this moment, Cody Carnes is singing "Take You at Your Word." God was so clear as he prepared me for this current season. He told me to trust him, that the book you are reading was part of his plan for my life, and that he would equip, fill, and sustain me along the way. My phenomenal thirteen-year career in the classroom was preparation for the words on this page. Every student, every moment, was preparing me for this season of authorship.

For me, listening to Christian music created a habit of worship that satisfied my thirsty soul. When I was worshipping, I wasn't afraid. It's hard to worship in a fearful state. The blinding light of praise filled the empty spaces in my soul with things that are good.

God's Word is available in a wide variety of formats, all at our fingertips. This verse assures us that any time we consume his truth, we are filled with good things. We can all relate to hunger and thirst, and we know that filling ourselves with empty calories is a short-term fix that will not sustain us for long.

When we examine our daily fuel source, what do we find? It may be Christian music or something else, and that's okay. Whatever it is—a daily verse, a motivational podcast, a pastor on social media, a devotional reading like this one—does it leave us feeling satisfied and full? If it's rooted in God's Word, our tank is sure to be full to overflowing.

God sent his message through songs to satisfy my soul when I needed it most. In a lonely and uncertain season, God's message of hope and encouragement filled me with song.

Rooted

When we fill ourselves with the good things of God, his goodness will overflow into our lives and fill our classrooms.

Refreshed

Reflect on your preferred fuel source and its ability to fill your soul with things that are good.

37
Walls of Self-Control

Like a city that is broken into and without walls so is a person who has no self-control over his spirit.

Proverbs 25:28

Behavior issues. The overarching bane of the teaching experience.

If you ask any teacher—elementary to high school—to name the number one behavior issue in the classroom, most of them (if not all) would say "excessive talking."

From the beginning of my career, I knew I wanted an amazingly productive yet quiet classroom. A tall order for any teacher, but especially for today's educators, who are plagued by the microscopic student attention span.

At the beginning of my career, I developed a strategy centered on self-control. Instead of using harsh rules and consequences to demand that students remain quiet, I decided to appeal to personal responsibility with a common goal—fabulousness.

We established this classroom mission on the first day of school. We would be as fabulous as we could possibly be, bell to bell. We accepted ourselves as fabulous, because that's who we are. This applied to every student in the room, no exceptions.

Each person oversaw evaluating their own fabulousness and adjusting their behavior accordingly, to build the walls of self-control. Once established, self-control is a fortress. When faced with the opportunity for distraction, students simply asked themselves, "Is this getting in the way of my fabulousness? I can do anything I set my mind to, including changing my behavior. I prefer to be fabulous rather than experience failure."

Once everyone understood their role, I introduced the cost-benefit analysis. What is the cost of talking throughout class and making no progress on your artwork? Talking, as a human activity, is not bad or wrong. Good conversation among peers builds healthy relationships. The time for that is at lunch and before or after school, but not in this class.

I taught drawing and painting, both of which require intense focus. Surprisingly enough, once the students understood the benefits and the work they produced as a result, quiet became the norm. We became a group of people who decided to be the best we could possibly be . . . quietly.

After a few years, our reputation for quiet prompted visitors to our classroom. Administrators would stop and peek into my classroom to see the anomaly for themselves—thirty-seven kids working in silence. Their look of awe was always the same.

The teacher next door asked how Johnny could be so quiet and focused in my room and talk nonstop in their class. Their room had no mission for success and no focus on self-control, only harsh consequences for the smallest infraction. Just as this verse describes, it was a city without walls.

Don't get me wrong—walls are compromised from time to time. Behavior that threatens the mission, unchecked by the student, requires intervention—personalized seating, grade adjustments, parental contact. Prior to these measures, there is a chance for redirected self-evaluation. The fortification of self-control is always the first line of defense against unsteady city walls.

We are all in need of a fortified city of self-control. Remember how I said focused self-control contributed to our mission of fabulousness? This behavior doesn't only apply to the students.

As teachers, we are constantly reflecting and evaluating everything in our practice, from strategies to procedures. These practices will keep us honest about the strength of our city walls. We can evaluate our self-control only to realize we need a redirect toward fabulousness ourselves. It's humbling, but if we don't address it, we extend an open invitation for the Enemy to break into our cities. The last thing he wants is fabulous success in our classrooms.

No matter the desired behavior, let's start with self-evaluation that builds strong walls of self-control. A fortified city promises success for everyone in the classroom.

Rooted

As we maintain self-control in all areas of life, we fortify the city walls of our heart and mind.

Refreshed

Reflect on the idea of self-control and how it affects the strength of your own city walls.

38
Graceful Forgiveness

In Him we have redemption through His blood, the forgiveness of our wrongdoings, according to the riches of His grace.

Ephesians 1:7

High school shenanigans. We've either witnessed them or participated in them.

In 2021 I led a freshman homeroom with twenty-three boys and seven girls, and I navigated my fair share of shenanigans. Living with a man who acts like a middle schooler most days has its advantages. Thankfully, my threshold for an angry response is high.

What we often fail to remember is that these ninth graders were middle schoolers three short months before they entered high school. This subset of the population could use a little extra forgiveness.

I'd attempted different behavior strategies in the face of shenanigans, but most effective by far was full-coverage forgiveness, with a sprinkle of name-calling (the good kind) for good measure.

We had a large courtyard in the center of our school building. It was sunny and bright, with metal picnic tables and benches. It was a popular lunch spot with the students, and we were fortunate that our classroom had courtyard access.

One warm and breezy spring day, a group of freshman boys was lunching at a table just outside my classroom door. There was lively conversation, boisterous laughter, and overly animated slap battles. As I sat at my desk by the window, I could see the rambunctious mood escalating.

If you teach middle or high school, you can almost sense when a situation is headed off the rails. Just as I was about to rise and open the door, the train derailed. A carton of milk rocketed through the air, meeting my plate-glass window with blunt force. The milk splatter was impressive, if I do say so myself.

I walked outside to see the boys admiring the milk splatter covering the entire window. All six froze, waiting for my reaction. By this time a crowd of onlookers had approached, both to admire the handiwork and witness the fallout.

"Gentleman, may I ask a huge favor?"

Silence and nodding. Lots of nodding.

"Would two of you please follow me into my room so I can get you a bucket of water and some towels? The hot sun is about to turn this milk into a stinky, crusty mess, and it's making it difficult for me to see out and enjoy this beautiful day. If you could work together to clean it off quickly before it dries, I would greatly appreciate it."

Wait. No principal? No call to parents? Not even a reprimand?

"Yes, ma'am. We are so sorry. We got this. We'll clean it up. Sorry. Guys, get the bucket." All of them spoke at once and scrambled to get up.

As they cleaned the window, I returned to my desk. The crowd outside dissipated—well, this was no fun. No Snapchat op here.

This incident could have easily escalated into me screaming, the principal appearing, everyone ending up in the office, parents called, and referrals written.

Likewise, God could just as easily give us what our sin deserves. But he doesn't. He offers a ransom for our souls through the precious blood of Jesus.

"Choose your battles" is a common buzz phrase in education. Discipline issues are not always minor, and some require serious action. I found that approaching the lesser infractions with grace and forgiveness helped push the Reset button and show students that this behavior is not who they are. Taking this forgiveness and transferring it to behavior issues can have a powerful impact on student behavior. These young men were "gentlemen," even though their puzzled looks when I addressed them as such said otherwise.

And the name-calling? What if we addressed students with names that align with who they are in the eyes of their Creator despite their actions?

When we survey what God has done for us, the magnitude of his grace can be difficult to digest. Just as he graciously forgives us, we can offer forgiveness to these young and inexperienced humans during their momentary lapses in judgment. It's fun to watch their faces when we don't react as they expect.

That group of gentlemen made the picnic table outside my room their permanent lunch spot. And from that day forward, all the milk remained safely on the table.

Rooted

Consider God's forgiveness as the precious gift it is—a beautiful testimony to everyone we forgive.

Refreshed

Reflect on a situation when your reaction to bad behavior testified of God's love and forgiveness.

39
A Unified Bond

In addition to all these things put on love, which is the perfect bond of unity.

Colossians 3:14

The field of education is filled with diversity, and not just among the students.

No matter how eclectic the staff, the perfect bond of unity is a love for student success.

I came to education late in the game at the age of forty-one, as fresh and green as a snap pea. The Enemy tells me all sorts of lies, and his choice lie in this season was, "You're too old and inexperienced. This job is gonna eat you alive."

Thankfully, God's hand placed me in a classroom next to a veteran teacher named Natalie.

Natalie had been teaching art for ten years. She was (and still is) insanely creative, and her energy knows no limits—she operates in overdrive at all times.

Our first meeting is still fresh in my mind. I can still see her perched on the end of a desk in my empty new classroom, legs swinging back and forth, baseball cap on backward, long blond hair in a ponytail, talking a mile a minute.

As she gave me the lowdown on all things school related, she cautiously inserted snippets of her personal life into the conversation. I could tell she was nervous as she offhandedly mentioned that her girlfriend also worked at the school as an English teacher.

"That's cool. My husband sells overpriced window treatments." We laughed out loud—the first of a thousand moments of laughter to come.

We became fast friends working side by side in the art-room trenches. The more we talked, the more Natalie opened up about the daily struggles she faced on the job.

Unbeknown to me, educators in Natalie's position live in a constant state of angst. With each semester, a fresh new fear arises that parents will discover her lifestyle and pull their child from her class. Or worse, they will file a complaint with the principal or superintendent about her position on staff. I was disheartened to learn that coworkers were often cruel and, in many cases, indifferent.

God's character is one of an all-consuming love for every person he created—there are no exclusions. As his followers, we are called to extend this love to everyone.

Education is trench warfare on so many levels, and we need to be unified in the battle. I wanted Natalie to know that God loves her and is always with her. As an ambassador to the King and as her coworker, I was always with her too.

No matter how we may feel about another person's lifestyle, God calls us to love one another. There are no descriptors on who is deserving or undeserving of this love. If God doesn't discriminate, by what authority do we? The educational ship is under attack from a multitude of outside factors. We can't afford to tear it down from within.

As teachers, acting in love toward coworkers shows our students unity among the people invested in their success. I attended a graduation ceremony once where the entire staff—principals, teachers, and support—lined the sidewalk, cheering and applauding as the senior class walked to the stage. The unifying love for that senior class was felt by all. I remember thinking, *Wow. What a blessed group of seniors. Every faculty should be united like this.*

Let's focus our energy on unity rooted in love, regardless of who is in the classroom next door. We can put on God's love like a garment for everyone to see, not just the people who share our same beliefs. We share a love for helping students, and when this love extends to our coworkers, our effectiveness as educators is strengthened. With God's love as its foundation, a faculty is built on the solid rock.

My friend Natalie had a hubcap from a late 1970s model truck hanging on the wall in her classroom. Shiny, round, and silver, with large black "GMC" letters in the center. Halfway through the semester, she told me how she had listened to one of my pastor's messages online, and it brought her hope for how God felt about her.

"Fox, when I look at this hubcap, the letters GMC make me think 'God Must Care.'"

Yes he does, Natalie. He most certainly does.

Rooted

What a blessing we share when we demonstrate a unified bond of love toward everyone, not just a select few.

Refreshed

Reflect on a situation when you had the privilege of helping someone see that God's love is meant for all of us.

40

Rejoice, Do, and See

I know that there is nothing better for them than to rejoice and to do good in one's lifetime; moreover, that every person who eats and drinks sees good in all his labor—this is the gift of God.

Ecclesiastes 3:12–13

Industrial floor cleaner. A sinus assault unlike any other.

The smell never failed to open my sinuses as I entered our school building.

My room was halfway down the corridor, and I never locked the door (sorry, not sorry if my former admin are reading this). No matter how early I arrived at school, there was always at least one group of students in my classroom, catching up on last-minute homework or just hanging out.

We treated the space like our home. A welcoming and secure place to be creative, supportive, and take risks. An atmosphere of excellence where everyone—including me—worked toward our established mission of being fabulous.

I entered the room with the same greeting every day—a loud and boisterous "How's it going?" I had been accused on more than one occasion of being far too lively at such an early hour. My enthusiasm was as real as it gets. In thirteen years of teaching, I had never approached that door with anything less than pure joy.

As class began and students filed in one by one, I would hear, "How are you doing today, Mrs. Fox?"

"Fabulous! I get to be here in my favorite place with all of you! Who's better than me? Nobody." At the beginning of my career, this response was me praising the answer to a ten-year prayer for my own classroom. I had waited so long to teach high school. As time went on, I realized how much this response helped shape my students' view of themselves.

I couldn't wait to get there and witness their growth, both artistic and personal. What a privilege to be alongside these students on their journey to adulthood.

A person at birth is like a block of smooth marble—perfect and unmarked. As the years pass, the marble is slowly transformed by family, friends, teachers, pastors, youth leaders, strangers—each one taking turns in sculpting the marble. Teachers have the unique privilege of assisting in shaping hundreds (or thousands) of young humans into successful adults.

When we look at our students, who are we in the presence of? The cure for cancer? The developer of a lifesaving vaccine? The winner of the Nobel Peace Prize? Influential people go to high school prior to asserting their influence. Think about it. Somebody was Martin Luther King's high school teacher.

What a privilege to be entrusted with God's children, people on a path toward their destiny. This is a genuine reason to rejoice in our profession. I know—I'm painting a grandiose picture, but God has established grandiose plans for all of us from before we were born. He has established each of our lifetime so we may rejoice in our work, all of us who eat and drink (that's everyone, by the way).

Teaching is a lifetime labor of love, a career not for the faint of heart. When we recognize the gift God has given us, to contribute to the finished forms of thousands of children, the responsibility is mind-blowing. Without teachers, there are no other professions. Every childhood dream begins during the school experience, and that experience begins with a teacher.

If you're struggling today, rest in the fact that in the first seat by the door sits a child who needs a capable sculptor. If the chaos is great and the job feels overwhelming, return to the reason you chose this path. Let's rejoice in doing good, knowing we all have but one lifetime. A lifetime of ministering to God's children in the classroom.

Rooted

We can rejoice and do good in every precious moment of this profession, and as we do good, let's choose to see the good as well. It is all around us.

Refreshed

Reflect on a situation when you've rejoiced and seen results materialize from doing good.

41
See the Goodness

I remain confident of this: I will see the goodness of the Lord in the land of the living.

Psalm 27:13 NIV

Sight is fickle.

We either see things through our own lens, or we allow others to tell us how to see.

If we're not careful, we will see our students through the lens of someone else's experience.

In February 2020, five weeks into the semester, a new student appeared at the door of my drawing class. My first instinct was annoyance. This class had hit its stride as a productive community. I didn't need the apple cart on its side because somebody couldn't handle calculus and needed out.

Because I know that each student is placed in my class on purpose—God's purpose—I took a moment and re-centered my focus. I introduced myself and told him to sit tight—his time to be fabulous was about to start. My promise brought only a confused look.

As I sat down to take attendance, I found an email from his counselor. She apologized for the late entry into my class, but they had no place else to put him. "He's just returned from a placement at the alternative school, but don't worry, he won't do much work for you and he won't cause any trouble." The words made my heart sink.

An entire synopsis of a young man's character in one sentence.

I walked over and pulled up a chair next to him. We were in the middle of a pen-and-ink life drawing of draped fabric. We discussed his experience with life drawing, which was minimal. After a quick drawing demonstration, I told him, "I'm glad you're here, and you're going to be fabulous." I handed him the pen. He thanked me and proceeded to draw with undivided attention for the next seventy minutes.

This next paragraph is one I am ashamed to type.

I was genuinely surprised that he worked so hard. One sentence in an email had shaped my entire view of this young man, and I saw him contributing little or nothing to the class. I had allowed someone else's vision and experience to cloud my sight. As the weeks went on, the humbling continued as he showed up on time, ready to work and be fabulous.

On March 7, 2020, we started a weeklong spring break that did not end for eighteen months. The global pandemic removed the students from my presence. The only thing remaining was an ugly gray container in front of the school to collect completed assignments. Opening that lid and seeing student work was the highlight of my day.

Drawings were to be dropped off on Tuesdays by 9:00 a.m. At exactly 9:00 a.m., I anxiously opened the lid, hoping to see beautiful artwork—it was the only goodness I could see at the time. Sometimes this young man's drawings were the only ones in the bin.

Shame on me.

It's not uncommon for teachers to share rosters before school starts, hoping to get the lowdown on whom we're about to encounter. I made it a point after this experience to never share another roster.

We will remain confident when we see the goodness of the Lord in the land of the living, not when someone else tells us what they saw. How much goodness have we missed already by seeing a student through someone else's eyes?

In the land of the living that is your classroom, imagine a roster that fills you with confidence as you see the goodness in every student on the list. A list that you keep between you and God until you get to know these divinely appointed students. Seeing their goodness transfers your confidence to them. They may even begin to see what you see—potential.

We can be confident of this: If we are breathing, we will see the goodness of God. Everything we see is his original design, created for us. Regardless of what or who we see, we need to be careful to view it and assess it through our own lens. Our lens, focused on his goodness, not someone else's lens.

Rooted

Remain confident in God's goodness. It is evident in your classroom, in every student you see.

Refreshed

Reflect on a time when God personally showed you the goodness in your classroom through your own lens.

42
Hearing & Doing

But prove yourselves doers of the word, and not just hearers who deceive themselves. For if anyone is a hearer of the word and not a doer, he is like a man who looks at his natural face in a mirror; for once he has looked at himself and gone away, he has immediately forgotten what kind of person he was. But one who has looked intently at the perfect law, the law of freedom, and has continued in it, not having become a forgetful hearer but an active doer, this person will be blessed in what he does.

James 1:22–25

If teaching is practice and practice makes permanent, the question becomes, What exactly are we practicing?

Are we practicing the love of Christ?

I've been in classrooms with "Safe Space" signs on the door, but where teachers tell students they hate the entire class. I heard a teacher once tell students she got paid whether they passed or failed. I've seen the hurt on kids' faces even as they act like these words don't matter.

A bad mood, personal issues right before school, or a lack of caffeine can derail our ability to respond with grace. It takes a calculated effort to establish a classroom safe space. One cutting remark can begin to unravel the confidence of an entire class.

God tells us here to be "doers of the word." The Bible gives us clear direction about our speech. As believers, our call to action begins with kind words. We gain nothing by speaking harshly to others, no matter how irritated or overwhelmed we become.

In my classroom there were students who, no matter how thoroughly I explained the assignment, followed me back to my desk immediately afterward, paper in hand. "Mrs. Fox, I'm confused. I don't know what to do."

I would bet my salary that you're picturing at least one student right now. This question can rattle the most patient teacher. No matter how we choose to respond, the student is not the only recipient. Our answer is heard by everyone. Our teaching practice, for all to see and hear.

In the early years of teaching, I heard this unnerving question frequently. I was obviously in need of a new strategy for giving directions, one that would eliminate student questions and decrease the risk of an ill-fated negative response.

I decided to have the students jot down all assignment directions in their sketchbooks or project notes. They switched papers when we were finished to make sure their table neighbor had written the directions correctly. Almost overnight the number of times I heard "I don't know what to do" went from every day to once a week, if that. I also discovered that collecting everyone's notes at the end of the semester for an exam grade made energetic notetakers out of the most apathetic students.

When students write down the directions, they are much more apt to retain the information. Hearing is a temporary act, and what is heard is easily forgotten. Writing is "doing." It's no different for us. We need to hear God's Word and act on it. This passage says that hearing without acting is like seeing ourselves in a mirror, walking away, and forgetting what we look like.

It is easy to forget God's Word in the midst of a tense student interaction. This muscle memory requires practice with intention. Practice makes permanent. Once ingrained, we can easily respond to our students as God so graciously responds to us, with kindness in the face of frustration.

I know it seems trivial, this story about a repetitive question. Teaching is a mentally and physically exhausting profession, with the potential for tiny cracks in our resolve. It's the little things that often trip us up. We hear God's Word calling us to act in kindness and grace toward others. The Enemy searches for these tiny cracks to create opportunities to weaken our resolve and our "doing" of the Word. If we remain centered on actively practicing what we hear God speaking, the smallest annoyances will have no power to derail us.

Rooted

When we practice God's commandments in our classrooms, we strengthen our witness as we show our students his grace.

Refreshed

Reflect on a time when God called on you to not just hear, but to be a "doer" of his Word.

43
Higher Ways

"For My thoughts are not your thoughts,
Nor are your ways My ways," declares the Lord.
"For as the heavens are higher than the earth,
So are My ways higher than your ways
And My thoughts than your thoughts."

Isaiah 55:8–9

The most difficult days are when we find out a student is no longer with us.

No matter the reason, the heartbreak is profound.

This morning I received word that a former student died yesterday of a brain tumor. Thirty-two years old, he was in my homeroom at the beginning of my career. His infectious smile and kindness toward everyone is permanently ingrained in my mind.

I wish I knew why things happen the way they do. Why do some people see ninety years and others only see thirty-two? We will never know why this side of heaven. Of one thing I am sure—each student is a gift, destined to be with us for a God-ordained purpose.

I do not believe in happenstance, only divine appointments. Whether a student is a joy or a threat to our sanity, each one is in the room for a reason. Maybe instead of assuming we will all be around indefinitely, we could spend more time in each moment. Rather than focusing on our plans and desired outcomes, maybe we could break our days into small moments of student focus, approaching every word with a Christ-centered purpose. Acting as we know Jesus would in every classroom interaction.

We presume to know where we'll be ten years from now. Truth is, we don't know what the next ten minutes hold. Back in 2012 I thought the students in my homeroom would all live to see many decades ahead. As it turns out, three of them are no longer with us, including that kind young man who just left us yesterday.

Our earthly plans are full of limitations. Our thoughts take us to places of inadequacy as we focus on our limitations and question our abilities. Thank goodness God does not see us as we see ourselves. He sees endless potential, and he has given us the Holy Spirit to guide us along the way. His thoughts are for us to be the very best version of ourselves. The statement in verse 8 is a declaration that his ways are higher; his method and manner for bringing us to our calling is not often aligned with ours.

Even though our plans often shift course unexpectedly, we can rest on this promise. God's ways are greater and higher, and his timing is perfect. As the heavens are higher than the earth, so are God's ways higher than our ways and his thoughts higher than our thoughts. These verses remind us that the maker of the universe thinks about us, cares for us, and promises to lead us along the pathway of life. What it doesn't say is that we will always understand God's methods or his timing.

I thought I would be in my classroom forever, laid to rest on my desk, surrounded by adoring students lamenting my passing. I thought that the young man from my homeroom would grow old, living out his calling (he had become a successful high school teacher and basketball coach). Instead, here I sit in this quiet room, typing this devotional entry, mourning his passing while my granddaughter sleeps, living out the unexpected calling of coming alongside you with classroom memories and God's promises. Needless to say, things didn't go as I had planned.

The peace we experience when we trust God's ways transcends all understanding, and that's how we can know for certain that his ways are higher than ours. Our classrooms are filled with his divine appointments. He has placed us exactly where we need to be, doing exactly what he has called us to do, even when we don't understand his plan. Receive the blessing of every student who walks through the door, knowing that God has a plan for each one, and he's allowed us to be a part of it.

Rooted

Rest in the fact that even if it doesn't make sense, God's ways are better; they offer us indescribable peace and purpose.

Refreshed

Reflect on a season when you gave a situation over to God and accepted his manner and method as better.

44
Holy Spirit, Come

But He said to them, "It is not for you to know periods of time or appointed times which the Father has set by His own authority; but you will receive power when the Holy Spirit has come upon you; and you shall be My witnesses both in Jerusalem and in all Judea, and Samaria, and as far as the remotest part of the earth."

Acts 1:7–8

This entire book is a testimony to the presence of the Holy Spirit.

If you had asked me five years ago where I would be in 2025, I certainly wouldn't be doing this. I would still be in room 357, surrounded by amazing high schoolers, watching them make phenomenal art.

Teaching high school was my dream job, and it was a gift straight from the hand of God. I was blessed to teach for thirteen years.

Had I known my teaching career would be over so soon, I probably would have spent most of it agonizing over my short tenure, dreading the last day and missing all the joy. I was blessed with a wonderful principal, a thriving art program, a hearty budget, and a ten-minute commute to school. I spent every Sunday evening looking forward to Monday.

Tiffany, I want you to write a devotional for educators.

"That's okay. I'll pass."

God's all-knowing sovereignty keeps us safe from ourselves. We simply don't need to know everything. Had I received this call eight years ago, I would have sprinted in the other direction like my hair was on fire. I was perfectly content teaching art, thank you very much. God, being who he is, had other plans.

A series of divinely placed events set the wheels in motion—our daughter starting a family, the housing market exploding, the growth in my art-curriculum business. About a year after the move, I finally surrendered and sat down to write. I was terrified. I didn't know what to write or how to write it. I'm not a writer—I'm a teacher. A wise and dear friend said to me, "Rather than focus on what *you* want to write, invite the Holy Spirit in and ask him what *he* wants you to write."

"Well now, isn't that an interesting approach?" Duh.

So I did. I invited the Holy Spirit into the devotional.

"What do you want me to tell them, Lord?"

As he brought story after story back to mind, I prayed for the perfect verse from the Bible to accompany each one. I'm no Bible scholar, as you may or may not have noticed. I love God with all my heart, mind, and soul, and I love teaching. Looking back, I understand now why I needed to trust his calling. God's presence, wisdom, and guidance covered me from my first college class in 2001 to my first teaching position in 2009. Those thirteen years teaching art equipped me to move into a new calling—coming alongside fellow educators, staying rooted and refreshed daily in God's presence. Were it not for my faith and God's leading, this journey would not exist.

The message in the verses above is clear: We're not supposed to know how or when God's plans will evolve. This is a gospel story of God's love for us and his care over us. In the verses above, the disciples were about to take the good news of Jesus to the ends of the earth. Like us, they are anxious for answers regarding his return. We are often anxious about his answers and responses to our own situations. We don't need to know all the answers.

The gospel went out to the nations one person at a time, one story at a time. This book evolved one story at a time. Your school year will progress one day at a time. Remain in the moment and seek the Holy Spirit's guidance for every student and every situation. Trust in his miraculous abilities. He is faithful to fill you with his power so your testimony is effective in all you say and do.

Once we invite God in, he remains in our hearts, filling us with his Holy Spirit to bear witness of his love to our students. We are fully equipped for the job, regardless of what we think or feel. The power of the Holy Spirit lives within us, and there is much work to be done.

Rooted

The Holy Spirit dwells within us and prepares us to live out God's calling on our life.

Refreshed

Reflect on a time when you experienced God's peace, releasing the fear of the unknown as you invited the Holy Spirit to work in your circumstances.

45
Shared Comfort

Blessed be the God and Father of our Lord Jesus Christ, the Father of mercies and God of all comfort, who comforts us in all our affliction so that we will be able to comfort those who are in any affliction with the comfort with which we ourselves are comforted by God.

2 Corinthians 1:3–4

In my first year of teaching, on the day we returned from spring break, a young lady named Katherine was late to my class. Halfway through the period, I looked over to see her standing in my doorway, a blank expression covering her face. If I close my eyes, I can still see her. She motioned me to come out into the hall. I approached her slowly and said, "Honey, are you okay? What's wrong?"

"Mrs. Fox, I'm not sure how much I'll get done in class today. My dad died over spring break."

This is one of those sentences that leaves you speechless. I hugged her. She didn't cry; she was so quiet and still. I scrambled for the right thing to say, but the Lord prompted me to stop. She didn't need to hear my words. She needed my presence.

I walked her into the room and helped her get settled. She was clearly in shock. I assured her that not only did it *not* matter how much work she completed, but if she needed to leave to talk with her counselor, she was not to ask—just go. I stepped out of the classroom and called her mom. It was much worse than I could have imagined. Her father had taken his own life.

I asked her mom if it was okay to share my own story with her daughter, as I had traveled a similar path. She gave her okay.

I told Katherine about my twenty-six-year-old cousin who had violently taken his life when I was in high school. I confessed that I had no idea what to say, back then or now, but that I would be praying for her and her family. If she or her mom needed someone to talk to at any time, I was available.

Katherine took me up on my offer later that week. I applauded her courageous efforts, showing up to school in the midst of her pain. She confided that she was afraid for her mom. There had been no forewarning of her dad's decision. The entire family was firmly in the grip of shock and disbelief.

Of all the things I imagined dealing with during my first year teaching, this felt like a trial by fire with no water in sight. Needless to say, Katherine struggled the rest of the semester. When staying focused was too difficult, we talked about strategies for moving forward in the midst of her grief. God provided me with wisdom and words for every conversation, sharing my experience when appropriate, but mostly listening. There were many impromptu visits to her counselor.

It's not always a good idea to share personal information with students—there is a fine line between what is appropriate and what is not. In this case one of my students was facing the darkest days of her young life, and we shared a tiny piece of common ground. I had watched my family grieve the loss of my cousin, watched them lean on God in an effort to survive the horrifying circumstances.

I wish I knew why bad things happen. There are just some things we will never receive answers for on this side of heaven. What we do know is our God is a provider—Jehovah Jireh himself showers us with comfort in every difficult circumstance. Our students will face unspeakable hardships while in our care. Our source of comfort is also their source of comfort. These verses tells us he is the Father of mercies. When we navigate a difficult or tragic life event, he is right there with us, carrying us through the storm. We can share our story with our students and their families, coming alongside them and reflecting God's love as we support them in their time of need. A beautiful picture of how

God uses his people to cover all of us in his grace, fulfill his plans, and fulfill his purpose.

Rooted

We can trust that the Father of mercies is pouring out his endless comfort on us so we are equipped to help our students deal with hardships.

Reflect

Reflect on a time when unspeakable hardship came into the life of a student and God used your story to provide them with comfort and support.

46
A Kind Environment

She opens her mouth in wisdom,
And the teaching of kindness is on her tongue.

Proverbs 31:26

Good vibes make for a productive classroom.

The words in the air shape the vibe in the room.

When students enter our rooms, how is the air? Anxious? Angry? Calm? Fresh?

An air of kindness builds a legacy of security that students remember forever. I received this note from a student in my art foundations class.

"Mrs. Fox. Every day since the first day I stepped foot in this class on the first day of this school year, I have never been happier to be in school because I have never seen someone be in such a good mood to teach a classroom full of kids."

This particular class was one of my largest, with thirty-seven students. Fourteen of them were freshman boys. A strategic operation in classroom management, to say the very least. To make matters more challenging, that semester was our first time back from the pandemic with all students on campus. Welcome to the jungle.

Anxiety was high, attention spans were short, and behaviors spanned the spectrum from halfasleep to bouncing off the walls. For many students, their guard was up and their walls were high. I needed a consistent strategy steeped in kindness.

As they approached my class each day, I opted for an extra-exuberant welcome, complete with open arms, high fives, and a lot of boisterous arm movements. While I may have appeared slightly unhinged to my seniors (they loved it but would never admit it), the freshmen thought it was hysterical. When you feel welcome in any space, the tone is set for a successful visit.

When I heard my name (as we all do, five hundred times a day—and sometimes in our sleep), I responded with a genuine "Yes, dear?" The post-pandemic anxiety in the room was palpable, and this approach seemed to soften the air. It's natural to assume that our students receive kind words from all the adults in their lives. I remember that a few of the students seemed unusually surprised at the kind response directed their way. It made me wonder if they were a stranger to kindness elsewhere.

"Mrs. Fox, I was blessed to be in your class. Due to Covid, I and many others didn't like coming to school, but your class made it worth it. I wanna thank you for encouraging me and making me always do better, even when I didn't think I could."

From time to time, students asked me why I never yelled at my pupils. It seemed like an odd question, and my answer was always the same. "You don't yell at the people you love." Raised eyebrows and looks of *hmmmm* followed. A reminder of what they could continue to expect. No further explanation needed.

Proverbs 31, verse 26, is part of a series of ten verses centered on God's description of a capable wife. He describes all her noteworthy attributes, and in this verse the attributes of wisdom and kindness are spoken in the same breath. God views kindness as a form of wisdom. With kindness at the core of our teaching style, students are guaranteed to experience wisdom every time they enter our classrooms. The result is a peaceful environment that welcomes students and guarantees success for every student.

As Jesus followers, we are called to emulate God's love for people. In our classrooms, the priority is kindness toward our students. Every time we hear our name (even if it's the five hundredth time), we have the opportunity to respond with a kind word. God calls us chosen, beloved, and friend, just to list a few of his endearing terms for his children, and he never tires of responding when we call his name. We are in the business of responding to God's children, and kind words fill the air with the security students need to learn.

Rooted

Kind words shape the tone and tenor in our classrooms. Words that bring our students peace, if only for a short time.

Refreshed

Reflect on a day when a note from a student reminded you of the power and influence of your kind words.

47
Parental Support

She watches over the activities of her household,
And does not eat the bread of idleness.
Her children rise up and bless her;
Her husband also, and he praises her, saying:
"Many daughters have done nobly,
But you excel them all."
Charm is deceitful and beauty is vain,
But a woman who fears the Lord, she shall be praised.
Give her the product of her hands,
And let her works praise her in the gates.

Proverbs 31:27–31

With thirty-plus kids in a classroom, we overhear a wide variety of student conversations.

The moral dilemma often arises between what to address and what to let go.

Just before Mother's Day one year, I overheard a young lady complaining about her mother. Evidently, in this student's opinion, the mother in question had fallen short on her duties. The laundry list of offenses was long and colorful. As the complaining continued, other students chimed in with similar stories of maternal shortcomings. I approached the table, stood quietly, and waited until the uncomfortable "teacher presence" settled in. When it was my turn to talk, I began my approach carefully, in a deliberate and quiet voice.

"So tell me—what is the thing that annoys you the most? Is it the clean clothes that appear in your room every few days? Is it the way the lights come on every time you flip the switch? Maybe it's the refrigerator full of goodies. Or the way your phone is always on and in service?"

Silence.

You see, I knew the mom whose daughter started the complaint campaign. This woman was in postgraduate school to become a high school principal. An exhausting educational journey with a steep incline—steep for people who have only themselves to care for. She also had two other children and was working full-time.

"There are only twenty-four hours in a day. Once your mom is finished with work, she has to make sure that your family has food in the house, clean clothes in the drawers, and that all the bills are paid. On top of that, she has the constant concern of your and your brother's whereabouts, safety, and care. All this comes before she even begins to think about working on her postgraduate work. I'm guessing that happens once you are tucked into your nice clean bed for the night."

The silence following a mic-drop moment is powerful. Four sets of eyes, wide and staring at me like they had just been caught kicking a puppy.

I am fond of this passage of Scripture for several reasons. The entire dedication from verse 10 to verse 31 is devoted to the worthiness of the hardworking wife. I'm going to speak to my ladies specifically, but if you are a man reading this, don't check out. I want you to picture the hardworking women in your life. No matter their role, when we read God's praises over their work, it can serve as a reminder of how much these women need our human support too.

Teaching is an extremely challenging profession, a job both mentally and physically exhausting. Whether we are teaching while raising a family, teaching with grown children, or teaching with no children, we're all tired. We need one another. As we support and encourage our female coworkers, we value them as God values them. The Lord is specific in his glowing description of a woman committed to her husband and family. His view is no less praiseworthy if we are raising a family alone.

We are the hands and feet of Jesus. Let's lift up our moms (and dads!) and find practical ways to show our support. There is no better testimony of the love of Christ than helping others. If we keep our eyes open, we are sure to see an opportunity to lighten someone else's heavy load. When we outwardly support our coworkers, our students witness the acts of kindness firsthand.

Rooted

As we humanize parental responsibility with our students, we offer them a chance to see their hardworking parents with a fresh perspective.

Refreshed

Reflect on a time when you acted as the hands and feet of Jesus and lightened the load of a hardworking parent coworker.

48
Value and Worth

So he said to him, "What is your name?" And he said, "Jacob." Then he said, "Your name shall no longer be Jacob, but Israel; for you have contended with God and with men, and have prevailed."

Genesis 32:27–28

I have a thing about making sure students feel valued.

Some methods are obvious, others are more subtle, and some are totally unbeknown to me until after the fact.

Regardless, the message is simple: You matter, and I'm glad you're in my class.

One year I had the bright idea for an acrylic painting lesson in which we painted giant disco balls. It was right before Christmas break, everyone was burned out, and we needed something relaxing and fun. My inspiration came from the electrifying disco-ball paintings by the amazing contemporary artist Sari Shryack. This seemed like the perfect idea for our intro to color theory.

As was customary, I made everything much more intense than necessary. I planned to have the students paint the disco balls on poster board—twenty inches in diameter. For beginning painters, this was quite large and intimidating. This particular group was slightly more energetic than most classes. Did I mention there were fourteen freshman boys? The disco fever was about to take the roof off.

I had visions of cutting out thirty-seven templates and then taking a chance on the transfer drawing onto the poster board going off without a hitch. It didn't seem likely. To save time (or so I thought), I drew out all the disco balls myself. After almost an hour, I leaned back and looked at the stack of poster boards, anticipating the chaos of thirty-seven students (in a room built for twenty-eight—remember those fourteen freshman boys?) all painting twenty-inch disco balls at once. I had a thought.

Make it personal.

It seemed odd since it was just a circle on a piece of paper, but all of a sudden I had an idea. I set up my phone to take a time-lapse video. I wrote each person's name, slowly and carefully, on the poster board just outside the border of their disco ball.

When finished, I watched the video and uploaded it to our classroom Instagram account. I added a teaser blurb of the painting excitement that was coming soon to my Art 1 Foundations class.

The next day the class came in buzzing about the Instagram feed. They rifled frantically through the stack of poster boards, searching for their name.

"Where's my disco ball, Mrs. Fox?"

"How long did it take you to write each of our names on all of these?"

We finished the project in record time, with no incident and with every paintbrush returned squeaky clean. Thirty-seven beautiful disco balls ended up on display for the entire school to enjoy. All fourteen freshman boys fully engaged.

It wasn't the painting project that was exciting as much as the thought of me taking the time to personalize each disco ball. An unintended message telling them how much they mattered. Something as simple as personalizing a lesson does not go unnoticed by students. A Crayola marker and a fifty-cent piece of poster board can make a person feel like a million bucks.

As teachers, we contend with pushback, behaviors, apathy, and lack of support. All this piled high on top of permanent exhaustion. Let's face it—the struggle is real. We have an example of perseverance in Jacob's wrestling match with God. This biblical throwdown reminded me of our struggles in the classroom and the agonizing weeks before holiday break. Reading this passage, I pictured the hours-long struggle, Jacob wrestling with the Lord from sundown to daybreak—with a dislocated hip, no less. God took the time to call Jacob by a new name, Israel, meaning "Let God prevail" or "God perseveres."[5]

God prevails in our classrooms every time we place the value on our students above all else. The lesson we teach may be amazing, but how do our students gain understanding of their personal value? We may not give them a whole new name, but when we prioritize their intrinsic value, the name we call them is "Worthy."

Rooted

God's love shines in our classrooms every time we value our people over the product.

Refreshed

Reflect on a situation when making your students feel valued inspired their behavior.

---

5. Doug Hershey, "What Does Israel Mean? Exploring This Important Biblical Name," Fellowship of Israel Related Ministries, November 1, 2023, https://firmisrael.org/learn/what-is-the-meaning-of-the-name-israel/.

49
Encouragement

For God has not destined us for wrath, but for obtaining salvation through our Lord Jesus Christ, who died for us, so that whether we are awake or asleep, we will live together with Him. Therefore, encourage one another and build one another up, just as you also are doing.

1 Thessalonians 5:9–11

Teaching can be a lonely profession, even with thirty-plus kids in the room.

Students are not mature enough to lean on, confide in, or trust with sensitive information—especially if you teach high school. We can be friendly with students, but it is not the best idea to be friends with our students (especially on social media!). Teenagers are too young and inexperienced for personal adult relationships.

Educators are natural collaborators. If you are the only person at your school teaching your content, the isolation can feel overwhelming. As believers, we are recipients of God's lasting salvation, and as a result, we are called to encourage one another. What a wonderful opportunity for us to come alongside our coworkers who are feeling isolated.

I'm a big-picture kind of gal, always looking to decipher God's plan regardless of my location.

"Why am I here? Is it about me helping the kids—or helping someone else?"

I made a decision early on to be on the lookout for the answers to these questions. Instead of keeping my head down in the hallway, I engaged with my fellow teachers and staff members, even if for a few minutes. A few questions beyond "How are you?" can reveal a hurt or a concern that could use the encouraging love of Christ.

When I really expanded my gaze outside my classroom, I discovered a building full of people in desperate need of encouragement. I found myself adding moms, children, and spouses to my prayer list. I listened instead of talking. I walked away from conversations feeling full and blessed that I had helped someone else's day become a little easier.

I didn't pretend to have all the answers, but I did have a kind word to offer and an ear to listen, even if it was only for a few minutes in between classes. As I left my classroom, I asked God to show me someone who needed encouragement, praying for wisdom and discernment as I walked the halls. Kind words are soothing, both to the speaker and the listener. I returned from the smallest conversations hearing God say, "They needed to hear that."

Sometimes I was the one who needed encouragement.

So many Spirit-filled moments flood my memory. Getting an update on a sick family member of one of our front-office staff (the real MVPs in education). Praying for the terminally ill wife of one of our amazing custodial staff. Brainstorming with our lead guidance counselor on ways to help our most at-risk students. Strategizing with the first-year teacher across the hall on creative ways to improve classroom management. Finding out that one of our teachers had a husband in the hospital, and dropping off a card to help her family buy groceries.

None of these instances were earth-shattering, but they were moments of encouragement that enabled someone to make it through the day. God has placed people all around us who need to see how much he loves them. Our salvation is the cornerstone of our encouragement. Because we are saved by God's gracious gift, we are called to share our gift as we build up others. Salvation is a gift meant for everyone. The most encouraging piece of news we will ever impart.

The educational workplace can be a sea of loneliness and discontent. When people are hurting, the tendency to hurt others rises. We know how wonderfully fulfilling it is to lift another person's spirits—it's how we interact with our students in our classrooms, and it's life-giving.

All these precious moments in the school hallways were divine appointments on God's calendar. Instead of focusing on the floor as we walk the halls, let's look up, watch for possible appointments, and show up.

Rooted

Keep your eyes open—the workplace is full of opportunities to encourage others.

Refreshed

Reflect on a time when you showed up for a divine appointment to build up a fellow teacher or coworker.

50
Ageless Witness

Let no one look down on your youthfulness, but rather in speech, conduct, love, faith, and purity, show yourself an example of those who believe.

1 Timothy 4:12

No matter your age or years of experience, the light of Christ can fill your classroom.

If you're entering the classroom at age twenty-two, thirty-two, or forty-one like me, God's timeless light fills each of us. It then searches for opportunities to illuminate the darkness.

Kids arc searching for truth in a world filled with uncertainty. If I were a betting person, I would put money on the fact that if you are under the age of thirty, your Jesus light is even more powerful. Youth carries a lot of weight, especially with teenagers. Enter the classroom adorned with the characteristics in this passage—godly speech, conduct, love, faith, and purity.

I taught in a public school for thirteen years, but that didn't stop me from filling my room with the hope and grace of Jesus. I took every opportunity to shine the light with every spoken word. Before we began a test, I dropped a quick "Don't worry, you'll do great. I prayed for you." At the end of the day, "Y'all be safe. I've got you prayed up."

Contemporary Christian music and sermon replays filled the room during my planning period. There were times when students wanted to come in and work on their art projects. They were always welcome, under one condition. "If you stay, you gotta listen to my Jesus music." No one ever left.

My church bumper sticker shined loud and proud on the side of my filing cabinet. Sermon notes covered the remainder of the same cabinet, carefully taped side by side, a wallpaper of spiritual refreshment. I often noticed students sitting at my desk combing over the information on the cabinet. I can only hope they were reading.

As a young teacher, the temptation is to be "cool." A word of friendly advice. Teens receive plenty of "cool," and most of it fickle—here one moment and gone the next. I realized early that students gravitate toward the teachers who provide a safe, secure atmosphere—especially one with high expectations and firm boundaries. If those boundaries were covered in kindness and grace, all the better. A classroom filled with God's life-giving characteristics is one so overcrowded that its capacity threatens to exceed the fire code.

This verse is referring to ministers, but I don't think it's a stretch to suggest that teachers are also ministers—one of our many hats. We shepherd young humans daily, providing for their needs as we guide them toward success. Our words and actions play to a highly impressionable audience. As believers, we are called to godly speech, conduct, love, faith, and purity as the leading characteristics of our teaching style. If each of these characteristics aligns with God's Word, the light of Christ in our classrooms will be positively blinding. As the teacher, it makes no difference how old you are. There are no age limits on godly characteristics.

This light can offer stability to our students, who crave it so desperately. Our witness provides calm in a chaotic world. A class period of safety, security, and peace. We've all had students ask if they could stay in our room all day. Not because we're cool. Ha! I was anything but cool. It's the feeling of security that brings the frequent request to stay all day. Whether it's the surroundings, the background music, or the lack of slicing speech, whatever they see and feel inside our classrooms draws them back for more.

Godly words and actions are both ageless and timeless. There is no minimum age requirement or years of experience to be an effective witness for God in our classrooms. We are never too young (or too old) to set an example for him. Our story of faith will permeate our classrooms regardless of whether we are young or not.

Rooted

Use your words and actions to shine God's light in your classroom. There are no age limits on godly characteristics.

Refreshed

Reflect on a situation when your godly actions transcended what you once thought were age limitations.

51
New Mercies

The Lord's acts of mercy indeed do not end,
For His compassions do not fail.
They are new every morning;
Great is Your faithfulness.

Lamentations 3:22–23

I had the privilege of teaching at an affluent suburban high school. While my job was free of budgetary restrictions, it was often plagued with personal tragedy. Privilege often comes with a cost. We all know the saying "More money, more problems."

It was not uncommon to have kids disappear off my roster for a stint in inpatient rehab.

As graduation approached, I often broached the subject of choices and their life-changing consequences with my seniors.

"One day in the future, our paths will cross again. As we chat, you will be telling me one of two things. Either how great college is and how well you are doing, or how you're bagging groceries at the food mart because things didn't work out as planned, and you're back home trying to get it together."

As much as they hated a lecture, this hypothetical scenario seemed to resonate.

During my first year teaching, I met one of the most talented young people to ever step over my threshold. He had everything most students only long for.

Handsome, from a wealthy family, with more talent in his pinky finger than most people have in their entire body. On the days that he came to school, his talent and creativity were unmatched. Because it was my rookie year and he was a senior, I only had the privilege to work with him for a short time before he graduated.

In addition to his positive attributes, rumors of extracurricular leanings circulated the staff lounge, most of them drug related. I had no definitive knowledge of their truth, but if they were even half true, his college experience was going to be rough. I remember praying, for his sake, that the rumors were false.

Sometimes all the classroom dialogue in the world will not stop a speeding train. When this young man was present, I decided to focus on his potential. We had several veiled conversations about choices and how they determine the difficulty or ease of our life's journey. Instead of thinking I was wasting my breath—advice from several coworkers—I prayed and poured God's truth into this young man. He has a plan for all of us. This child was no exception. He was present the day I gave my "One day I'll run into you again" speech. I may or may not have delivered it with a little extra oomph specifically in his direction.

Graduation came and went. In August I ran into him while he was shopping with his mother, a cartful of dorm room accessories in tow, ready to take on the world.

In January a fellow teacher informed me that my student had been expelled for conducting unsavory business transactions on campus. Several years later, I saw in the news that his older sister had been found dead in a hotel room in another state. She, too, was fighting the devastating demons of addiction.

As tragic as this story is, the bigger tragedy is this: If you are teaching middle school or high school, you can relate. As you read this, you're remembering a student of your own. It's heartbreaking to watch young people make these life-altering choices.

It's good to know that in the face of tragedy, we can rest in the daily promise of God's new mercies.

These situations provide fields ripe for the harvest. In this case, we discussed how precious both life and opportunity are and how the best plans can be obliterated by one choice. That each one of us is worthy of success, and destructive choices have no place in our lives. We can approach our students with a story free of judgment and full of concern for the precious life God has freely given to each of us.

I recently saw my former student on social media, clean and sober, fighting to regain his health, dedicating his fresh new journey of hope to the memory of his sister. When we watch former students overcome hardship—self-imposed or otherwise—we have a message of hope to share with our current students. We never know who is on the verge of making a life-altering decision and how a story of hope might change the trajectory of their life.

Rooted

In the face of devastating choices, God's mercies never end and are new without fail—every single morning.

Refreshed

Reflect on a time when you learned of a student (past or present) who overcame hardship and experienced God's new mercies and great faithfulness.

52
Online Grace

In everything, therefore, treat people the same way you want them to treat you, for this is the Law and the Prophets.

Matthew 7:12

When I was a kid, we were fairly careful with our harsh words about others for fear of this one phrase coming back through the grapevine: "Say it to my face."

Fast-forward forty years. Here we are, device in hand, playing keyboard cowboy on social media. Just because we're behind our phones doesn't exempt us from the words in verse 12. I'm old enough to remember life without social media, when a snarky or ill-timed comment fell on only one or two sets of ears. Today these same words have the potential to touch millions of lives. Depending on our mood while typing, the potential for harm is endless.

We want our children to be respectful and kind toward one another and toward adults. We vehemently discourage bullying of every sort. These children then get on TikTok, and what do they see? Adults being disrespectful, unkind, and bullying one another, all in less than ninety seconds.

To make matters worse, there is no guarantee of truth in anything we see. Information is contrived and conveyed through smoke and mirrors, veiled innuendo, and artificial intelligence.

I saw a social media post the other day that brought tears to my eyes. A parent had posted a video her son had taken of his teacher giving a lecture.

This teacher was of foreign descent, and their accent was strong. The caption on the video was this: "No wonder my kid is failing this class, the teacher's accent makes it impossible for him to understand the material." The tone was hateful and cutting. It broke my heart.

As it turns out, this wasn't the teacher's real voice at all. The voice had been dubbed over with a strong accent. Someone who had actually been in that class commented on the post, expressing what a wonderful teacher this person was and how sad they were to see this. They were devastated for the teacher, as the video had hundreds of thousands of views.

As if this single incident isn't sad enough, there are countless educators, administrators, and parents taking shots at each other on social media platforms. And yet we want our own children and our students to treat everyone with respect every time they pick up their phones.

It's just as easy to type kind words as it is to type nasty ones. Our fingers move over the same set of keys. As believers, we are rooted in the love of Christ. We have an opportunity to shine that love throughout the world with our online presence. What if every time we begin to type, we ask ourselves, "What will this bring in return?" We have the opportunity to bring a smile to a face we will never lay eyes on. When others see our social media posts, they can be confident that if they stop scrolling and read, they will come away feeling better than they did ninety seconds ago. What a gift God has given us in the ability to communicate his love and mercy with the entire world.

God wants us to sow kindness and grace, both in person and online. Seeds of hope and light going forth all over the world from our devices. Regardless of how we feel about a random school-board decision, a two-hour delay for students, or an unexpected school closure, we can pour out kindness into the online space toward our administration, students' parents, and community members. We are ambassadors for Christ, witnesses to his saving grace, speaking his love and mercy into the world for all to hear (and read). What a privilege to reach an entire world with this glorious news.

Rooted

Let's take every opportunity to stop the scroll with words of love and kindness, spreading the love of Christ with every post.

Refreshed

Reflect on a moment when you stopped scrolling long enough to share God's love with the online world.

53
Return on Investment

Sow your seed in the morning and do not be idle in the evening, for you do not know whether one or the other will succeed, or whether both of them alike will be good.

Ecclesiastes 11:6

Education is the purest form of human agriculture.

I like to picture the lady in the chicken yard (stay with me—this is going somewhere) scattering seed from her apron by hand, tossing it in all directions, hoping that the chickens will feast on what she has to offer.

Teaching is a constant flurry of intent and action—we are everywhere, all the time, doing all the things, hoping our students will feast on the knowledge and life skills we offer.

There are a million teaching strategies out there. We've all endured painful professional-development sessions on most of them. Some things in life are best taught by doing. If we want to teach a skill or task that lands with purpose, we demonstrate it.

Hard work is under attack in our culture. I see people online constantly telling me I can write a book in a weekend. That's rich. As I type this sentence, it's been two years since I began this calling.

I always enjoyed working alongside my students—I might have been cleaning, organizing, or hanging up artwork, but I was rarely stationary. I also worked a side hustle designing, sewing, and rhinestoning competition bikinis for bodybuilders. I know—it was as niche as it gets. I often woke up at 3:00 a.m. to sew before school. The students were constantly asking me about the business and how I could possibly manage it alongside teaching.

Coffee. Copious amounts of coffee.

There were lofty expectations in my room. Not just for the level of effort that goes into creating art, but also for how we invested in our goal of excellence. This place was special because the people in the room were focused on excellence. We were on a daily mission to be the best we could possibly be. All of us—me included.

We spent a considerable amount of time discussing investment versus return.

"If we spend our time doing nothing, what do we get in return?"

"Nothing."

This statement is a famous Foxism. One year the kids taped a large piece of paper to the wall and wrote their favorite Foxisms. This one showed up several times on that paper.

Helping students understand the concept of time—and how to get the most out of the time we have—is key to their success. Time management is a life skill. If we want our students to be consistently productive, they need to see the adults in their lives living productively.

"Mrs. Fox, do you smoke pot?"

It's high school. We get *all* the questions.

"Every day I am blessed with a new twenty-four hours—that's if I wake up. If I smoked pot, I wouldn't have the energy or clarity required to accomplish all the fabulous things I get the privilege to do every day, like being here with all of you. And I would probably sew through my finger."

The looks on their faces were priceless. They were expecting a pot lecture. Instead they heard about the gift of time. Not gonna lie—I was also secretly hoping for a shift in their view of the return on their potential pot investment.

This verse and its message of working day and night does not negate our need for rest. There is a time for rest; God is very clear on this issue. Goodness knows, in the current state of education, teachers are short on rest. Taking care of ourselves through rest enables us to fully engage when it's time to work hard.

Outside of our daily responsibilities, God has provided us time to pursue our dreams. This verse tells us that we don't know which of our efforts will succeed, but it says that one or the other—or both—will. Whether it's a side hustle or a retirement gig, he has opened the windows of time.

The message here is one of daily perseverance and commitment. God has given us breath in our lungs and the time to pursue our profession and our dreams. What a gift to approach this job with diligence. We share a testimony with our students in the midst of our perseverance.

Rooted

Hard work is a heart posture of thanksgiving for the breath in our lungs and the time to pursue our calling.

Refreshed

Reflect on a time when you saw students embrace hard work as a result of witnessing your diligent work ethic.

54
Prepared

When my anxious thoughts multiply within me,
Your comfort delights my soul.

Psalm 94:19

"Dude, I am *so* nervous. I'm so gonna fail this math test."

We've all heard it, this declaration of impending failure.

"Did you study for the test?"

"No."

"Well, of course you're going to fail. You're not prepared. No wonder you're so nervous."

"If two people are in the same building and both need to use the bathroom really bad, but only one of them knows where the bathroom is, who is more likely to be anxious?"

"That's easy! The person who can't find the bathroom."

Finally, logic students can understand.

My final exam is taken art-survey style, complete with a 120-slide PowerPoint and a blank answer sheet. Students spend several weeks preparing for it the old-fashioned way, with a handwritten study guide and a set of flash cards made from index cards—old-school style.

My sales pitch was also old school. "If you write it down, you are much more likely to remember the information."

Exam prep was actually a lot of fun. Cutting and pasting tiny pictures of famous artworks, gluing them to the cards, and then writing the information on the back. We always enjoyed coffee and donuts on flash-card day.

One of my favorite things to do was patrol the classroom with my garbage can, stopping at each table and scooping up the paper scraps. I'm full of nervous energy, so for me it was something to do while they worked. I circled the room over and over, slowly and carefully collecting the trash. As I made the rounds, I noticed the students sitting up straighter, cutting more precisely, and writing with careful intent as the air of confidence increased.

The confidence came in knowing they would be prepared for the final exam. It was a difficult test, intended to mimic a college-level assessment. In the beginning they were anxious about passing, wondering how they would ever remember all the artworks and artists. Then they discovered that the path to success is paved with preparation. A study guide, flash cards, review sessions. As they completed the steps, the anxiety dissipated, until exam day, when they entered the room, flash cards and study guide in hand, ready to rock and roll. You could feel the confidence in the room. It was electric.

As we teach our students how to prepare academically, we show them how to remove anxiety and replace it with confidence. With confidence comes comfort in knowing they are prepared. God offers us the same comfort with his presence and his Word. Both provide preparation for us to remove anxiety from our lives. God is Jehovah Jireh, our provider. We can draw on this endless supply to release the pressure valve on our anxiety. His supply never runs out.

The endless job requirements in education can be overwhelming, especially if you are new to teaching. As believers we can delight in comfort that defies anxiety. We can prepare our hearts by spending time with God, reading his Word, and praying in his holy name. As we grow closer to him, we see our confidence increase and our anxious thoughts dissipate. The result? Comfort.

When the situations around us multiply our anxious thoughts, we can take comfort knowing that God will provide everything we need to handle whatever we face. Our job is to actively pursue his comfort by preparing to alleviate the anxiety. We've all been there. That feeling of total peace in the midst of the anxiety. This is the comfort described in verse 19.

As the students finished their flash cards, their smiles were always big. "I'm *so* gonna ace your final, Mrs. Fox."

Rooted

Prepare your heart as you draw closer to God and watch the comfort wash over your anxious thoughts.

Refreshed

Reflect on a time when you prepared your heart and God brought delightful comfort in an anxious situation.

55
Humility

When pride comes, then comes dishonor;
But with the humble there is wisdom.

Proverbs 11:2

Pride is the great equalizer. A powerful force that carries with it the potential to change the course of our lives.

Occasionally we encounter students who appear to be unteachable. They showed up already "amazing"—they've heard it their entire young life. The wall between them and new information is strong.

One of my favorite teachable moments is a story from my college experience. It was the year 2008, and I was forty-one years old and in the final year of my art education program. I was taking Art of the Mexica (properly pronounced *Mu-shee-kah*). The class met in the evening, and I lived thirty miles away. I had a daughter in middle school and a husband who traveled for work every week. I needed the course to graduate. I was annoyed from the outset.

The professor—a twenty-six-year-old woman fresh out of graduate school—assigned a five-page paper. We were to examine and evaluate a piece of Mexican art and speak to its cultural relevance. My composition met all the requirements and was submitted on time. It was a captivating read from start to finish.

When the paper was returned, it had a large red C- next to the title, along with a handwritten note: a recommendation that I read Strunk & White's *The Elements of Style* to improve my writing. Evidently I was too "wordy." What

I was, was annoyed. This lady was half my age. Her lack of experience and maturity had obviously clouded her ability to appreciate my writing style.

She graciously granted me a chance to resubmit the paper. She was even willing to expunge the C- and replace it with the second evaluation. Talk about grace. But there I was, stewing the entire drive home, my pride in overdrive.

As I fumed, God began to speak. Let's face it. I hadn't written a paper in twenty years. Maybe this was a divine appointment. The next day I bought *The Elements of Style*, read it, and rewrote the paper. As much as it pained me during the entire process, I received an A on the rewrite.

Whenever I shared this story to my students (and I shared it every year), I referred to my attitude as a "baby fit." That's exactly what it was. Me digging my heels in and refusing to be taught. Once I got over myself and listened to God speak humility over my situation, the rewrite was easy.

What I didn't know at the time was how pertinent this experience was to God's influence in my future classroom. Students never failed to listen in awe as I admitted my ego trip steeped in pride. Maybe they weren't used to soul-baring honesty from other teachers. The rich classroom discourse that followed my confession served as a teachable moment as I relived it and they received it.

The takeaway? "Everyone has something to learn." Once we release our pride and prepare our minds to accept the learning, we can accomplish anything.

God gives us the chance to learn every day. We honor him when we humble ourselves and accept good teaching. When we share humbling experiences with our students about our own journey with learning, they see it's okay to admit we still have much to learn. That professor opened my eyes to how much I needed to learn about writing. God used a humbling situation to prepare me to write the book you are reading today.

We honor God every time we lay down our pride and opt for learning. Learning to follow him can be a humbling journey. As we shift our attention away from our desires and spend time in the Bible, in prayer and reflection, we grow spiritually. All these learning habits draw us closer to God.

Humility is part of everyone's journey, young and old. As I type this, I am so thankful for that young professor. She has no idea how God worked through her to bring you and me together.

Rooted

Remain in a constant state of humility, one that honors God with a readiness to learn.

Refreshed

Reflect on a time when you chose humility after God revealed a pride issue that threatened your ability or willingness to learn.

56

Timely Wisdom

So then, be careful how you walk, not as unwise people but as wise, making the most of your time, because the days are evil. Therefore do not be foolish, but understand what the will of the Lord is.

Ephesians 5:15–17

Time is a difficult concept for teens to understand. At the age of sixteen, time feels endless.

In December 2012 the Scholastics Art and Writing Competition was fast approaching. We had five students competing, each preparing an eight-piece portfolio. One young lady in particular, Dana, had an incredibly strong body of work—large, vibrant colored-pencil portraits showcasing a variety of emotions. Amazingly prolific work for a person so young.

The competition deadline was January 15. The week before holiday break in December, Dana came into my room, sat down in front of my desk, and started crying. *Sobbing* is a better way to describe it. She was always so calm and focused that this alarmed me, to say the least.

"Mrs. Fox, I can't do it." The tears would not stop.

After a few moments, she calmed down enough to tell me she didn't have time to complete her last three drawings for the competition portfolio. My heart sank, as I was convinced she had both regional and national awards in her future. She explained that she had a new boyfriend, and between school and the portfolio, she had little to no time for him. He wasn't a fan of his place on the food chain.

The thinnest ice we walk on as educators is choosing the words to motivate a teenager.

After a quick prayer and a deep breath, I told her about time. About investment and return. About how January 15 was coming whether she spent time with the boyfriend or with her God-given talent. I told her about drawings she would have forever (one of which now hangs in my foyer). I reminded her of aspirations she had to attend an architectural program and how this work would also serve as her entrance portfolio.

I finished by asking her to reflect on her boyfriend's support. To honestly ask herself if he shared her dreams. If he did, he would still be there on January 16 to congratulate her on her submission and share in her success.

As adults, this is a question we can ask ourselves. Do the people in our lives share and support our dreams? I don't think it's too much of a stretch to consider God's input on who we keep company with. How do they affect our time management? Do they want us to succeed, as God does?

The Lord has gifted each of us with talent and opportunity. His hand is evident in our current location, whether we are still in the classroom or venturing into uncharted waters. Wherever we find ourselves, our biggest asset is time. This is our life currency. We honor God when we choose to spend it wisely.

Time is the common denominator for all people, the only thing we all share equal amounts of. God equates wisdom with making the most of our time. His will is for us to honor his gifts and grow the talents he gave us. This growth begins with honoring the gift of time. If we can teach our students the importance of effective time management, they will leave our classrooms equipped and ready to fulfill their dreams.

On a crisp sunny day in March, I celebrated as Dana crossed the stage and received her awards. She walked away (boyfriend-free) with more regional awards than any other student in the eighteen-county cohort. In May she received a National Silver Medal and a $1,000 art-supply gift card.

Eleven years later, Dana is now a successful architect.

Rooted

Consider the value of time and its capacity for us to pour out our God-given talents into our dreams.

Refreshed

Reflect on a situation when you helped students understand the value of time and shared in their hard work and success.

57
Compassionate Forgiveness

Be kind to one another, compassionate, forgiving each other, just as God in Christ also has forgiven you.

Ephesians 4:32

Picture a ringmaster in a big tent circus commanding the movements of thirty-five performers while standing on one leg.

Now imagine the audience criticizing the show every time a performer misses a cue.

That's teaching.

In order to keep the criticism to a minimum, communicating with the audience—otherwise known as our students' parents—is key.

My August parent letter set the stage for the semester ahead. Everything from expectations to grading criteria to supply lists, it was a fairly intense letter requiring a parent/guardian signature under the "I understand all of it" statement.

There is nothing worse than a parent email that begins with "You never told me . . ."

Parents were fully aware that my final exam was worth 25 percent of their students' final grade—that signature came in handy in the few instances when they claimed ignorance.

One year, exam day came with an unfortunate incident. Everyone had turned in their flash cards, and manila folders were turned up on their sides around each person's answer sheet. We called this building a "safe house" around your intellectual property. The lights were out and the projector was on, queued to the first slide.

With each new slide, I noticed a student toward the front of the room hunched over, the sound of paper rustling, and taking an unusually long time to write his answer. The students around him looked nervous. Without a word I walked up behind him, reached over his shoulder, and took the stack of flash cards from his hands. And on to the next slide we went, without a word or a reaction.

At the end of the exam, the flash-card shuffler approached my desk.

"Mrs. Fox, I am so sorry, and I have no excuse. I didn't study. Can you please let me retake the exam? My dad is gonna kill me."

We both knew that his parents would be less than impressed with his test-taking ingenuity. Our exam makeup day was slated for Friday, which usually served as a quiet workday for me, as I rarely had students needing to retake the test. This in-person retake for one unprepared student did not sound appealing.

The humility it took for him to admit his failure without one lame excuse hit home. How many times had I been in a similar place and been granted a second chance by a gracious and loving God? More than I cared to admit.

"Be here at 8 a.m. ready to go. The first slide will be up on the screen at 8:05."

On his course evaluation at the end of the semester, this young man wrote, "Mrs. Fox has showed me tools that I will use forever." I'm hoping one of those tools was forgiveness.

In January 2024 I received a message from a young lady who had remained in contact with the young man who'd successfully retaken my exam all those years ago. Just after the holidays, he had succumbed to the demons of substance abuse, three days after leaving a forty-day rehabilitation program. She wanted me to know how much he loved me and the time he spent in my class, and that he spoke of me often.

God provides avenues for us to extend grace to our students every day. Whether we are ignoring the tardy bell for a student who works late to help support their family or allowing someone to retake a test, our posture of grace leaves a lasting impression. We are often unaware of that impression. Let's rest in God's posture toward us, emulating his love and extending grace in every manner possible. Planting the seeds of forgiveness among our students helps them see God's love in action. Seeds that will grow to maturity as they leave our classrooms and forgive others.

Rooted

Plant the seeds of compassionate forgiveness throughout your teaching practice, knowing the lasting effects of this grace on your students.

Refreshed

Reflect on a situation when you extended grace and forgiveness to a student in need of a second chance.

58
Strong and Safe

The name of the Lord is a strong tower;
The righteous runs into it and is safe.

Proverbs 18:10

What type of building houses your classroom community?

Is your classroom a strong tower? Do you call on God for a place of refuge?

My classroom teaching style was based on a model of God's grace, offering students an atmosphere of safety. Just as God desires to leave us better than when he found us, I desired to leave my students better than how I found them. I also wanted them to feel safe in the process. They might leave my class a better artist, a better listener, or with a better view of themselves. No matter the outcome, better in a safe space was the goal.

In year one of my teaching career, on the first day of my second semester, I noticed a new but familiar face in the classroom. A young man at the back, hood up over his head, sitting quietly and attempting anonymity.

"Michael, what are you doing here? You were in this class last semester."

"It's okay, Mrs. Fox. My counselor said I could stay."

Don't forget, it's my first year in the classroom. I barely know how to take attendance, much less what the rules were for repeating classes—by choice. Was that even a thing?

A quick phone call to the guidance department revealed that a brand-new counselor was handling this young man's schedule. That made two of us who had no idea what the rules were. In the flurry of last-minute schedule changes and at his request, she had enrolled him in my Art 1 class. She completely overlooked that he had already taken the class—and passed with an A. He interpreted her reenrollment as "No problem, you can take the class again."

"Why do you want to take the class again? You've already done all the work. You'll be bored."

"It's nice here, Mrs. Fox. I like it."

Lest you think this man wanted to stay because my class was easy, I can assure you it was not. In fact, I'd been accused of taking my Art 1 class way too seriously. A freshman boy once told me, "This is *not* Art 1, Mrs. Fox—it's more like Art 7." He was painting his multihued twenty-inch disco ball using only the primary color and white, and smiling ear to ear as he said it.

I never learned the full details of why Michael wanted to hang around for round two of Art 1. Boys (young and old) tend to be aloof with their feelings. It's okay. It's not important why he wanted to stay. The fact that he went to all that trouble to enroll in my class again spoke volumes. Maybe he felt safe, or confident, or both. Hopefully both.

This verse assures us that the name of the Lord is a strong tower, and that those who run into it are safe. The verbiage is running, not walking. When life gets difficult, let's not waste time heading into the only place guaranteed to offer us safety.

Rather than relying on the opinions or feedback of others, we have the privilege of running into the strong tower of the living God every time we feel the urge to spew. Running into his presence guarantees us safety from the storms of life. The storms don't subside, but God gives us shelter as we navigate the waves. We can call on his holy name, run into his presence, and allow him to guide us safely through the trial and out the other side. This experience is indescribable. We are shielded all around, as if nothing can harm us. God is with us in our classrooms, a strong tower of strength. We can teach from a place of safety as we model this strength for our students. A learning environment filled with God's presence provides our students a place to experience his protection, a classroom filled with peaceful productivity.

Rooted

When we call on the name of the Lord and run into his strong tower, we provide a strong, safe environment where our students can learn.

Refreshed

Reflect on a time when you called on the name of the Lord and went running into his strong tower to build a safe classroom space for your students.

59
Stress Management

The Law of the Lord is perfect, restoring the soul;
The testimony of the Lord is sure, making wise the simple.
The precepts of the Lord are right, rejoicing the heart;
The commandment of the Lord is pure, enlightening the eyes.

Psalm 19:7–8

We live in an age when everyone wants to be heard.

There is no shortage of platforms to spew our frustrations. It can feel therapeutic. How often do we search for answers in places that have nothing to offer us?

Education is ripe with reasons to vent. If it's not the students, it's the parents, the administration, lack of curriculum, staffing issues, or the latest school-board proposal.

We complain to our coworkers, friends, and spouses. We pop into online forums and craft lengthy and heated posts. These rants result in a temporary feeling of camaraderie that is unlikely to be sustained. Spewing our discontent into the online space invites and breeds discontent. Sure, we may find someone to offer support and occasionally a solution, but the majority of responses are filled with anger—misery loves company. The onslaught of opinions, many of which are not fully informed, offer a limited ability to encourage us.

Encouragement is restorative and wise, filling both the person giving and receiving it with hope.

When I landed my first job teaching high school across town, my daughter asked if she could leave her current high school and come with me. A sixteen-year-old girl and her forty-one-year-old first-time teacher mom heading into a brand-new school together. Uncharted waters for both of us. It was pretty scary.

On our first day of school, my daughter surprised me with that jar full of handwritten Bible verses. "I thought this would be good to help you when you're feeling scared." She had seen me fight my way forward for seven years on my journey to the classroom. She was also familiar with my high-strung personality. It was obvious I was a nervous wreck. That she had taken the time to write out each verse and place each one in this jar filled my heart with an indescribable peace.

The jar found a home on the windowsill by my desk. The pieces of folded paper were my lifeline, a constant supply of God's restorative truth at my fingertips. After a difficult day (or in the middle of one), instead of finding someone to listen to my rant (which on many days sounded much more appealing), I reached into that jar and pulled out a random verse. The verse never failed to align with the situation, and it always offered me much-needed refreshment. God has a way of putting his finger directly on the pulse of our need, restoring our soul with his Word. The verse above says that the Lord's precepts—his principles and commands—cause our hearts to rejoice. A jarful of rejoicing sitting right next to my desk.

When the stress becomes overwhelming and the complaints increase, we can go to God's Word for restorative refreshment. He offers us an endless source of wisdom in ways that are easy for us to understand. His wisdom and guidance quench our frazzled, thirsty soul with a peace that passes all understanding. Does this mean we experience immediate relief from our stress or find an instant solution to our problems? Of course not. Sometimes we wait, hoping to see God work on all the other people in the situation, and sometimes he does. Other times he works on us, enlightening our eyes to fresh new ways of thinking. He opens our eyes regarding our approach, our reactions, our assumptions, and our heart. He shows us the benefit of seeking him first.

Consider going to the wellspring of God's truth for peace in a tense moment. We can draw from it in any difficult situation, and the refreshing supply never runs dry. His Word freely offers us restoration of our soul, simplicity in his wisdom, and endless rejoicing for our hearts.

Rooted

Bring your concerns to the Lord before all else. His words will restore your soul as they bring wisdom and rejoicing, enlightening your eyes.

Refreshed

Reflect on a stressful situation in which you sought peace in God's Word first, and in the process discovered a joy-filled restoration of your spirit.

60
Calming Consistency

Now when Daniel learned that the document was signed, he entered his house (and in his roof chamber he had windows open toward Jerusalem); and he continued kneeling on his knees three times a day, praying and offering praise before his God, just as he had been doing previously. . . . Then the king was very glad and gave orders for Daniel to be lifted up out of the den. So Daniel was lifted up out of the den, and no injury whatever was found on him, because he had trusted in his God.

Daniel 6:10, 23

"What are we doing today?"

That one annoying question . . . frequently asked and forever irritating.

How could they not know what we're doing?! This thought raged in my head every time I heard someone ask it (pretty much every day).

Reflection is the foundation of the teaching profession. We plan, teach, reflect, adjust, then reteach. Personally, I tend to over-reflect in all areas of my life. This personality trait would come in handy during my tenure in the classroom. I had prayed far too long for this opportunity, and I wanted to give it my best. In the early days, something in my daily classroom procedures was causing confusion, and I needed to fix it.

As I examined my daily routine, I came to the realization that I didn't have one. Students were unaware of procedures and expectations because I hadn't told them. And if I did tell them, I lacked consistency. To make matters worse, the confusion was mostly among the students who needed extra support, and they were already anxious enough. Anxiety resides in the unknown, especially if we feel insecure to begin with. My lack of consistency was adding to their anxiety.

I was in bad need of a daily routine with clearly defined procedures and expectations.

I created a daily procedure in which I addressed the entire class with a rallying cry at the beginning and end of the period. We called it "Rallying the Troops."

1. Beginning of Class Welcome.
   "Thank you for coming to school. I'm so glad you're here."
2. Statement of the Day's Format.
   "Today will be a studio workday."
3. End of Class Wrap-Up.
   "Beautiful people, thank you for working so hard. I appreciate your fabulous efforts and amazing work ethic. Tomorrow we will take notes on our artist of the week."

Just like it says on the shampoo bottle . . . Lather. Rinse. Repeat.

A sense of overwhelming peace began to cover the entire classroom. Students entered the classroom expecting me to "Rally the Troops." At the end of class, students waited for me to wrap up and state the format for the following day. The number of times I heard, "What are we doing today?" reduced dramatically, and as a bonus, the "What are we supposed to be doing?" questions (equally as frequent) all but disappeared. My students with heightened anxiety were much more calm and productive. Added bonus: I found myself feeling more calm. As simple as it was, it was pretty miraculous.

Consistency offers a sense of security and alleviates anxiety. When Daniel feared for his life, he chose to pray out in the open, three times a day, just like he always did. He went to the Lord consistently in the face of impending death. What we face in our classrooms may not be life threatening (we hope), but we see here God's response to Daniel's consistent prayers—he shut the mouths of the lions. We can trust that God is faithful in our lions' den moments and in every other moment of our life. God's consistency alleviates our anxiety because we know we can trust him. When we offer consistency to our students in kind words, effective procedures, and endless grace, they trust us for a learning experience in a calm and smooth-running classroom.

Rooted

A consistent prayer life brings security in trusting that our God is faithful to answer us in his perfect will and timing.

Refreshed

Reflect on a time when consistency in your classroom resulted in peaceful productivity for your students.

61
Questions and Answers

I sought the Lord and He answered me,
And rescued me from all my fears.
Psalm 34:4

Running will either exhilarate you or exhaust you to tears.

In 2022 God began to speak to me about writing this book. His call went something like this: *Education is a sea of chaos and uncertainty. Teachers are frightened and weary. Tell them that I love them and that I am here in the midst of their classrooms, ready to help at any moment. They need a daily source of refreshment. They need hope. I want you to reflect on your time in the classroom and encourage them with my truth.*

I've never run so fast or ignored a call so deliberately in my life, and that's saying a lot.

I felt like that kid on the playground zigzagging back and forth to avoid being tagged. Remember how good it felt to form that letter T with both hands and yell "Time ouuuuuutt!" bent over, hands on your knees, sucking wind and trying to catch your breath?

That was me, and God had no intention of ending the chase, no matter how fast I zigged or zagged. The call was here to stay, resurfacing in my thoughts at the strangest moments. After a few months and a great deal of prayer, my focus shifted from "No way" to "What if."

What if I can write a book?

What if there are people who will actually read it?

What if?

As I near the end of writing this first book (a series is on the horizon), I've prayed over and completed almost ninety devotional entries, plus hours of author coaching. I should be elated, yet suddenly I'm terrified all over again. I know absolutely nothing about getting a book published. Zilch. Heck, I know nothing about writing a devotional (hopefully this isn't overly obvious).

Thankfully, my trust is not in my abilities. Like I just said, I know nothing about writing a book. What I do know is that the One who leads me as I write is the Lord of all creation. El Shaddai, which means "my supplier." Jehovah Jireh, "my provider." Every time I sit down to write, I invite the Holy Spirit to speak. As he leads, my fingers move across the keys and he reveals his truth to me in ways I never imagined. He pours out memories of endless joy from inside the walls of room 357. From the classroom to this calling, his presence is evident. With every sentence I type, he seamlessly connects the dots of my experience back to his provision and grace. He wants you to do the same thing. Connect your experience to his provision and see the good.

The word *seek* in Hebrew means "to search out by any method." I often have to ask myself, "What am I actually searching for?" If you had asked me five years ago where I would be today, it wouldn't be here, I can promise you that. Once I answered the call to write, God provided wisdom and words for every page. He led me to an amazing author coach and editor who helped me rewrite the entire book. Yeah, I thought I was finished five months ago. Wise counsel redirected me just when my ego was about to take a victory lap. What you're reading now is God's design, and his is so much better than mine.

God tells us repeatedly in his Word that if we seek his face, he will answer. Not always in the way we prefer, but he will answer. Because he loves us, his response—whether yes, no, or wait—will be better than anything we can ever imagine. Added bonus, he promises to rescue us from all of our fears. Not just some of our fears—but all of them.

If you are reading this and wishing you were anywhere else but where you are, please hear this. God knows your location, and you are there by his deliberate design. When we're not sure of our current assignment, we can pray and seek God's face and his direction. If we're running frantically from a call, we can slow down, call a timeout, and ask him for answers. We can rest in his promise to answer and deliver us from all our fears.

Rooted

What a faithful reassurance we have, knowing we can seek answers from the Lord in our professional life. His faithfulness is not limited to our circumstances. Seek him in the classroom.

Refreshed

Reflect on a time when you sought the Lord for answers and his faithful response provided direction and delivered you from all your fears.

62
Unexpected Seat Change

Abide in Me, and I in you. As the branch cannot bear fruit of itself unless it abides in the vine, so neither can you unless you abide in Me.

John 15:4 NASB1995

"Why do we have new seats? Are we in trouble?"

I was a huge fan of the unannounced seating shuffle—a classroom-management staple. No warning ahead of time. On any given day, students arrived to find themselves sitting in a new location. It wasn't a punishment for bad behavior. New seats allowed kids to get to know people outside their comfort circle. Students who were natural motivators had a chance to motivate the students in need of motivation.

Allow me to dazzle you with my high-tech approach. An overhead projector with a hand-drawn seating chart in Sharpie marker. (Under the age of thirty? Google "overhead projector," then go buy one on Marketplace. When the internet goes down, you'll be the only person in the building still teaching. They're also great for a no-prep negative-space drawing lesson—all you need is four pairs of scissors, paper, and a pencil. Low-tech skill building at its finest.)

Sorry. I got sidetracked.

Back to the unexpected seat shuffle. Early in the semester, this carefully calculated operation took more than an hour to plan and draw. Once I became familiar with the students' strengths, I could whip up a new seating chart in less than ten minutes.

The first time I rearranged seats, a young lady asked, "Mrs. Fox, how do you know where to put us? Is it random?"

I explained what I called "the method to my madness." How I carefully positioned each person where they could give and receive the most help. Students who shared hobbies and interests ended up at the same table, and people who seemingly had nothing in common often became friends, seen afterward having lunch together or hanging out before school. Because I had taken the time to get to know them at the beginning of the semester, along with their various gifts and strengths, the task was easy.

"Wow, you really put a lot of thought into this. That's pretty smart, Mrs. Fox. I wish all my teachers did this."

Comments in the beginning of the semester transformed from "Why do we have new seats?" to "We have new seats!" as the semester progressed. It was neat to see them excited about their new location, knowing the arrangement was well thought out. With no pushback, they gladly found their new seats, expecting to discover the reason for their placement.

In this verse God reminds us to abide in him, as he is already abiding in us. Close alignment with our Father enables us to bear fruit. God desires a personal relationship with us, one that involves spending time together in study and prayer. He changes our placement from time to time, sometimes unannounced yet always filled with purpose. When we abide in him, we can pivot in the change with hopeful expectation, confident that he is positioning us in a fruit-bearing opportunity. Whether personal or professional, accepting our new position and aligning our hearts with God's plan and purpose brings growth.

Investment in our relationship with God brings growth, and that growth brings with it the ability to evaluate a change in circumstances with a God-sized perspective. A "new seat" opens doors not present in our previous position. How exciting it is to know that the God of the universe will intentionally rearrange our circumstances to increase our growth potential. When we abide in him and sit in his presence, we are better able to respond with hopeful expectation, reflecting on his past faithfulness. God knows exactly where we should be, and we need not be afraid of things to come. His plans are precisely designed for our growth.

Rooted

Abide in God's presence. Seek his wisdom and guidance. Accept the unexpected seat change with hopeful expectation for an opportunity to bear fresh fruit.

Refreshed

Reflect on a time when abiding in God helped you understand and process an unexpected seat change in your life.

63
Words that Edify

Let no unwholesome word come out of your mouth, but if there is any good word for edification according to the need of the moment, say that, so that it will give grace to those who hear.

Ephesians 4:29

Spoken words remind me of toothpaste. Once out of the tube, there's no returning.

Our words shape the vibe in our classrooms. When students enter the room, how is the air quality? Anxious and angry? Or fresh and filled with hope for a great day?

One mouth to thirty sets of ears—a ratio capable of great impact.

During my career, our class mission was to lift each other up in both word and deed, giving grace to everyone. We viewed ourselves as a family—one filled with encouragement and respect, with no outsiders. As each semester progressed and students adopted this mindset, negative or unproductive words became almost extinct.

One day a student asked if she could step outside and return a phone call to her doctor. She was in therapy and had to change her appointment time. (If you're new to teaching, having students in therapy post-pandemic is quite common—it's also common for them to share this information openly.)

"Of course, honey. Do what you need to do."

A young lady at another table looked up from her work. "Mrs. Fox, why don't you get mad when someone asks you stuff like that? My science teacher flipped out on a kid who asked to make a phone call during class."

I had to stop and think about it. It was simple. At that moment there was no cause for flipping out. Besides, flipping out never helps anyone. An unwholesome response with unkind words would have derailed the entire trajectory of the class. The need for the moment was a compassionate approach to a delicate situation. The young lady needed to call her therapist. Like this verse says, a good word for edification was in order.

As it turned out, the student left the room, made the call, came back two minutes later, and went back to work.

"We have a job to do, and she had an important phone call to make. She asked permission to make a very important call, and I said yes. And we are still on the road to fabulousness."

She paused, thought about it, and went back to work. I could see that thoughtful look of *Hmmm, makes sense* on a few other faces as they continued to work.

Choosing good words not only edifies the person spoken to, but it also offers grace to those surrounding the conversation. When we speak good words to one student, twenty-nine others are listening. As a result, a blessing of grace fills the entire classroom.

This verse in Ephesians commands us to choose words according to the need in a particular moment. A word can be uttered in a split second. We face thirty thousand seconds a day in our classrooms, give or take a second. If we stay in the moment and monitor our speech, the chance for unwholesome words decreases considerably.

We can rest in the fact that if we ask, God will also give us words that address the situation and student need perfectly. When we are in the moment, there isn't room left for other emotions—worry over what happened five minutes ago, fear about what will happen in the next five minutes. We are right here, right now, seeking God's guidance and words for our next steps. When we choose words that edify, we build a stepping-stone of good classroom moments to follow. Responses based on God's guidance can't help but be filled with his goodness, paving the way for more good moments to come.

Rooted

Choose good words that build up every student in the room, regardless of whom you are speaking to, knowing that every set of ears feels the impact.

Refreshed

Reflect on a verbal exchange when you remained in the moment and spoke words of edification to a student, pouring out grace on everyone in the room.

64
Service

As each one has received a special gift, employ it in serving one another as good stewards of the multifaceted grace of God.

1 Peter 4:10

Teaching can feel thankless at times.

A career of constant giving—time, physical energy, emotional reserves, personal resources . . . the list goes on. You're nodding as you read this.

I experienced the most joy when I was giving the most to my students. Even when I thought I had no more to give, the more I gave, the more joy I experienced. Maybe this is a by product of God's anointing. He blesses each of us with the gift of service.

Honestly, it just feels good to do nice things for people, no matter who they are.

I'm a big coffee drinker. My collection of coffee mugs is impressive, and 80 percent of them were student gifts. We had a single-cup brew machine in our classroom. The students collaborated and purchased it for me at Christmas one year. It was red—my favorite color.

I spent the entire day with a coffee cup in hand, unless I misplaced it on a student's table, in which case I put out an all call: "Anyone seen Mrs. Fox's coffee?" I consumed my last cup around 3:00 p.m. If you've been in one of my workshops (online or in person), you are probably thinking I could use some decaf. I'm wired pretty tight.

Classroom coffee policy was to bring your own K-Cup and mug, and as long as you cleaned up after yourself, you could drink coffee during class. I know, sounds crazy, but I figured if it was okay for me to do it, why not them? It was high school, after all. Half the kids in my class were old enough to serve in the military within the year. Needless to say, they thought it was awesome.

One morning students were lining up at the start of class, K-Cups and mugs in hand, waiting patiently to brew their coffee. It was the end of the week, and we were all exhausted. There were at least six of them, and the wait to brew was sure to eat up valuable work time. I had a policy of bell-to-bell productivity, and they looked a bit nervous that they were in line for coffee and not working.

"Put your cup and your K-Cup on the counter and get to work."

The look of "no caffeine despair" was apparent on each face. They sadly but respectfully left their cups and returned to their seats. My intent was to make the coffee and bring it to each of them at their tables, but they had no idea. It took me a second to realize they thought they were in trouble.

"Oh no! I just don't want you to miss valuable work time! I'll make the coffee—I got you!"

Their reaction was priceless. As I made each cup of coffee, brought it to them with a napkin, and placed it carefully on their table, their thankfulness was one of awe more than anything. It didn't hurt that I had fourteen years of experience waiting tables. You never know when prior skills will come in handy. I think I even made a few server jokes. I never saw kids work so hard and enjoy coffee so much.

This verse commands us to serve one another. God loves us so much, and this love is manifested in our service to others. As teachers, we know how effortless it is to serve our students. We harbor a natural gift, whether it's to serve a cup of coffee or deliver a kind word during a math lesson.

God's grace is multifaceted. When the light of God hits the heart of our profession, the result is a service that is many sided. We all know the soul-filling joy of serving our students, watching them feel loved and cared for, and seeing them succeed. This is God's design, his calling on our lives. We are stewards of God's multifaceted grace. He meets our needs in an endless variety of ways. In turn, we are equipped to meet the needs of our students.

It feels good to meet a need. It feels even better to make someone feel valued.

Rooted

Teach with a servant's heart, approaching every act of service with the multifaceted grace of God.

Refreshed

Reflect on a situation when God's multifaceted grace was revealed through an act of service in the classroom.

65
Iron Sharpens Iron

As iron sharpens iron,
So one person sharpens another.

Proverbs 27:17

My first classroom was small. Over-fire-code-capacity small.

In a space designed for twenty-eight students, most of my classes usually housed between thirty-six and forty. Needless to say, we didn't have much room to move around.

Between the backpacks and the bodies, once everyone was seated, it was difficult to get back up. Hitting the bathroom before class was highly encouraged.

We had one pencil sharpener on the wall by the door. This was prior to my genius idea of handheld sharpeners and cups for shavings on each table, an invention bred from extreme overcrowding.

Honestly, I had waited so long and prayed so hard for a classroom full of students that I didn't care how many people they crammed into my room. Be careful what you wish for, right? Seriously, when my teaching position finally became a reality, my gratitude was so strong and my heart so full I didn't care how big the room was. I vowed to do everything possible to make these students feel welcome. I finally had my community.

It became painfully apparent that overcrowding would be an issue. Because it was an art class, supply distribution and functional art-making were difficult.

Just when the situation dampened my spirits, the Lord showed up to remind me how to use this tiny space to build a supportive community.

God is so good that he can remind you of his goodness with a dull pencil.

"Does anyone have a pencil sharpener I can borrow?" The quintessential art-room question.

As a student nearby attempted to open their backpack under the table, I reached for the dull pencil in his outstretched hand.

"I got you. Give it here. I'll sharpen it."

What happened next broke my heart. The look of awestruck unbelief is still fresh in my mind.

"*Are you sure?* No, Mrs. Fox. It's okay. I can do it."

First of all, no he couldn't. I prayed every day that we never needed to exit this room quickly.

"Of course I'm sure! How are you gonna be fabulous with a dull pencil?"

Once I had sharpened the pencil, I discovered that this simple gesture had sent a powerful message. With one simple act, the entire class knew I cared. They sat up taller and worked harder. What's more, if they did manage to make it to the pencil sharpener, I noticed them asking the people around them if anyone needed a pencil sharpened. Classroom community in action. While not my original intent, I was grateful for the effect.

God's Word tells us here that iron sharpens iron. His intent is for us to encourage one another, build one another up, and make life better for those around us. The metaphor is interesting because iron is a mineral needed for oxygen to flow through our bodies. We can't sustain life in our bodies without it. God has designed us to live in community with one another. In the same way, we can't sustain a community without encouraging one another. If we are to build a classroom mindset centered on success for everyone, our best bet is a foundation built on mutual support.

Joyfully serving others is a heart posture. When we approach our students with an attitude of humble service, we sharpen their view of how good it feels to support and encourage others. Our selfless actions offer them a framework for how to behave toward their peers and reveals to them the personal reward service brings. The encouragement is often in the little things, gestures we don't pay enough attention to. Sharpening a pencil seems like an insignificant gesture, but to some students it's the only nice thing that has been done for them in ages. A simple act with a powerful punch. Iron sharpening iron.

Rooted

Remain in a heart posture of humble service in your classroom, and watch a room full of sharp students emerge.

Refreshed

Reflect on a situation when your humble acts resulted in bringing a classroom community together with mutual support and encouragement.

66

Genuine Caring

But prove yourselves doers of the word, and not just hearers who deceive themselves.

James 1:22

"Don't act like you enjoy teaching if you really don't. Kids have a crap meter."

Single best piece of advice I ever received from a beloved middle school principal. This guy was a pro. He genuinely cared about the kids, and they knew it.

If you can work in a middle school without losing your marbles and the students love you, you've got mad skills.

Our school operated on a "SMART Lunch" schedule, allowing an hour for lunch, where students could eat anywhere in the building. On any given day there were at least forty people in my room at lunchtime. Thankfully, I had an enormous storage closet that doubled as a mini-lunchroom.

As you can imagine, with that many high schoolers in one place, shenanigans often occurred. One day my closet turned into an impromptu SMART Lunch vape lounge. Upon discovery and immediate closing, five students ended up suspended. The ringleader was a young man unfamiliar to me. The following semester, guess who appeared on my painting-class roster.

I could sense on the first day that he hoped I didn't remember him. Per department guidelines, students are required to take drawing before they take painting. It turned out that my vape-lounge ringleader had not yet taken drawing, taught by my colleague next door. I can't lie . . . I was relieved. But until his counselor could change his schedule, he was with me for the day.

As mentioned earlier, the first day of school is dedicated to learning all my kids' names and creating community. We played my corny name game, with me learning the first names and middle names of everyone in the room. We discussed siblings, pets, and hobbies. I showed them previous students' work and told them a bit about me as we established ourselves as a family of painters. I could sense my ringleader's interest growing over the course of the hour. He seemed surprised by my level of interest in knowing my students.

Once the meet and greet had ended, we had a few minutes left of class for casual mingling. My ringleader approached me with a sheepish look. "I don't know if you remember me, Mrs. Fox, but I was one of the kids vaping in your closet last year, and I wanted to say I'm sorry. I also wanted to ask if I could stay in your class. It looks like it will be really cool. I didn't take drawing, but I promise to work hard and not cause trouble if you'll let me stay."

Something (I'm sure it was God prompting me) told me I needed to allow him to stay. Every commonsense argument told me to send him straight to the schedule-change office, but God said, *No, he's here by my design. He also needs someone in his life who cares.*

Whoa. Point taken. No schedule change.

This young man ended up being one of the hardest-working students in my room. He showed up and showed out—every single day, without the vape. He even coined what ended up being one of our favorite painting-class phrases: "You can't paint scared." It's true. You can't. And to think that on day one I almost ejected him on a technicality.

Yes, of course we need to follow protocol when scheduling students, but every now and then God presents us with an outside-the-box situation where we need to walk the walk of grace. God's Word tells us to "do" God's Word, not simply hear it. Sometimes he speaks so clearly we can't help but listen. There are times when students enter our rooms in unconventional ways or inconvenient times. Instead of assuming the worst, we can look to God for his perfect timing. Sometimes when students arrive outside the normal channels of entry (and especially if they beg to stay), we can be sure God has a reason.

In most instances we have no idea what struggles our students face. We can be sure that we never go wrong acting on God's Word. Offering grace, a second chance, and an opportunity to be a part of a supportive community. As the hands and feet of Jesus, we show students how much God loves them. Our students thrive in a genuinely caring environment, especially a classroom where they see God's grace in action.

Rooted

Kids have a crap meter. They know we genuinely care when we are doers of God's Word, not just hearers.

Refreshed

Reflect on a situation when students saw God's love for them through your genuine acts of caring.

67
Something New

Do not call to mind the former things,
Or consider things of the past.
Behold, I am going to do something new,
Now it will spring up;
Will you not be aware of it?
I will even make a roadway in the wilderness,
Rivers in the desert.

Isaiah 43:18–19

When my husband and I decided to relocate in the middle of the post-pandemic housing craze to be closer to our daughter, everyone thought we were nuts.

Thankfully, God is always working, whether we realize it or not.

We called our Realtor on a Sunday, and ten days later we accepted an offer on our home, well over the asking price. The house wasn't even officially on the market.

While amazing, this blessing resulted in a tiny problem. We didn't have a house to move into.

We were two hours away, and every bid we submitted was outbid within the hour. With the market so volatile, we knew that if we were to find a home, God would need to show up in a big way. After three highly anxious bidding wars (that we lost) and no inventory to choose from, we made the decision on a Wednesday to relocate and rent until the market slowed down.

Twenty-four hours later we got a call from our Realtor. A beautiful home had just appeared on the multi-list at 10:00 a.m. Thursday morning. It was eight minutes from our daughter. (Our only deal-breaker was that we needed to be within a ten-minute drive.) Recent defeat had us believing that bidding was futile, but the house looked nice in the pictures and it matched our desired location, so we tossed our hat in the ring.

By the time we submitted a formal offer at 8:00 p.m. that evening, forty-six potential buyers had scheduled a showing over the next two days. At 9:00 p.m. the sellers accepted our offer and canceled all forty-six showings. By 10:30 p.m. we had purchased a home we had never stepped foot in. Talk about a twelve-hour move of God. Wow.

Less than a month later, on a trip to find an apartment nearby for my mother-in-law, we drove by the new house. The owner was outside, so I jumped out of the car and headed up the driveway. I've been accused of being forward, but sometimes forward comes in handy. I needed to know why she'd accepted our bid twelve hours after her house went on the market. Canceling all those showings and accepting our offer baffled me.

Her answer was straight out of verse 18. "Your offer was fair, and I had prayed up to this day that it would be clear to me who God wanted to buy our house. When my husband and I heard how you were moving here to be close to your daughter and her new family, we knew for certain that God wanted you and your husband to have our house."

Ever had a moment when you heard God's voice as someone was speaking? This was one of those moments. A response from a fellow Jesus follower that verified the last three weeks of whirlwind life-changing events. This was God doing something new right before my eyes.

Let's keep our eyes open lest we miss what God is up to. In verse 19 he challenges us: "Will you not be aware of it?" Pondering the things of the past requires time and energy. God is telling us to behold the new things—to appreciate and see that he will do something new. It doesn't say he "might" do something new. He will. We can rest in this definitive statement—new things are on the horizon. He loves us, and he is making a roadway for us to travel safely.

This is a story about a new house. Each of us is on the road to a new place, literally or figuratively. If we're returning to the same classroom in the same school for year number thirty-one, the experience will be filled with new people and new memories. If we're transitioning to a new grade level or a new school or out of education altogether, it is terrifying at the moment. Take courage and behold—God is the great highway engineer, making a way for all of us with life-sustaining waters of refreshment.

Rooted

God is making a roadway and a river in our new places, providing a means for us to travel and thirst-quenching refreshment along the way.

Refreshed

Reflect on a time when you found yourself in a new place, a new season, or a new relationship and God paved the way and provided the refreshment.

68
Whatever Is Good

Finally, brothers and sisters, whatever is true, whatever is honorable, whatever is right, whatever is pure, whatever is lovely, whatever is commendable, if there is any excellence and if anything worthy of praise, think about these things.

Philippians 4:8

Some students carry emotional weight that is heavy beyond their years. Our mission, while not always easy, is to meet them where they are and guide them toward safety and success. As believers, we show them the love of Christ along the way.

These are God's children, entrusted to us for a specific chapter in their young lives. There are no mistakes—every child is on our roster for a reason. When faced with challenges, the command in Philippians 4:8 is to focus on the good. We are to focus on whatever is true, honorable, right, pure, lovely, commendable, excellent, and worthy of praise. A beautiful description of the people in our care.

There are times when these beautiful people pull the veil back partially and give us a glimpse of a terrifying home life. When young ladies enter my classroom distraught and disconnected, offering silent innuendos of paternal situations too traumatic to speak of. Opening a student's sketchbook to read reflections on family dynamics that should never be written down. It was times like these when I needed to shift my focus to the attributes mentioned in

Philippians 4 and move forward with assistance when necessary. To remain in the circumstances without God's presence was too painful.

We face situations together that no group of young people should ever witness. I've arrived at school to hear of a student who took his own life in the bathroom at a school across town. The threat of an active shooter on our campus once derailed most of my painting class. Instead of painting, we spent most of class in a dark closet, hunched on the floor. Just two of hundreds of disturbing situations we can all relate to.

What about the horrifying situations we aren't privy to? Invisible forces that weigh on our students, tying them down as they strain to engage. What if every student came in with a piece of paper pinned to their chest—their burdens written in big, bold letters?

"Hungry. It wasn't my turn to eat this morning."

"Hurting. Physically assaulted by Mom just before school."

"Humiliated. Sexually abused by a family member last night."

Most times, if we really knew the evil we were facing, it would be too much for us to bear. Our students walk into school with any number of issues, with the weight so heavy it can only be carried by the power of Jesus.

The Enemy wants us cowering under the weight of such evil. We are the light of Christ in the midst of darkness. It's a focus issue. In the face of evil, we choose to focus on anything that is pure, favorable, and commendable.

As we focus on his goodness, God protects our hearts and minds so we can offer assistance. When kids show up each day burdened and fearful, we can encourage them with our focus, whether or not we know exactly what they are experiencing outside our rooms. We can look for and compliment all the good things we see, starting with their presence.

This verse says, "If there is any excellence and if anything worthy of praise, think about these things." There is always something excellent to think about. Showing up is excellent. Let's remind them how wonderful it is to have them in our classrooms. Given their circumstances sometimes, it's a miracle of God that some of our students not only show up but survive.

Rooted

Focus on all things good in the face of all things not. God is in it with you, no matter what.

Refreshed

Reflect on a time when you focused on God's attributes to help students see the good in an otherwise terrible circumstance.

69
Creative Solutions

I know how to get along with little, and I also know how to live in prosperity; in any and every circumstance I have learned the secret of being filled and going hungry, both of having abundance and suffering need. I can do all things through Him who strengthens me.

Philippians 4:12–13

Remember that small classroom I told you about a few days ago? Getting to the pencil sharpener wasn't our only challenge.

Lack of storage was a constant issue. Although I thought as the art teacher I deserved a bigger classroom (we've got a lot of stuff), I had yet to learn how classroom acreage often hinged on years of service (of which I had none).

So there. No big room for Tiff.

At least not today.

God has three responses for our requests: yes, no, and wait. Praying for a new classroom was not panning out with a yes, so I prayed for ideas and solutions. I also ramped up a thanksgiving campaign. Every day I made it a point to thank God that I even had a classroom packed full of students (literally). I also thanked him for his gift of good health to teach.

While my room number did not change, my perspective did, and creative solutions to various problems emerged. One of my favorites was a brand-new vantage point.

Using the digital projector and the whiteboard simultaneously was impossible, as they inhabited the same wall. One of my biggest challenges was delivering a lecture where everyone could easily see me. With the room's layout, it was nearly impossible.

On the back wall opposite the whiteboard was a countertop that ran the full length of the room. I don't know whose idea it was, but the custodian and I decided to paint a giant white square on the wall above the counter and pivot the ceiling projector 180 degrees. If I stood on the counter and directed one of the students at my desk to advance the slides (no remote control, unfortunately), everyone was able to see.

I saw nothing wrong with teaching from atop the counter. I ran back and forth along that countertop, talking about all things art and loving every minute of it. Was it the safest idea I ever had? Probably not. Safety schmafety—all I knew was every student could see! I had never taught high school before. I figured everyone taught from the top of the counter if the situation dictated.

Evidently this was not the case. The first time I jumped onto the table and over to the countertop, I turned around to see thirty-six shocked and surprised faces. I was so excited that I danced all over that counter, teaching like my hair was on fire.

"Mrs. Fox, what are you doing!?"

"Teaching!"

The secret to thriving in less-than-perfect circumstances is perspective. Once we shift our focus from the lacking to the blessings, we open ourselves to new ways of thinking. Hopping onto a countertop to overcome a space shortage is just one example. Thank the Lord I had a countertop. I'm sure you've solved many configuration issues with a creative idea or two. That's the heart and mind of a teacher. The environment doesn't have to undergo physical change for us to make a way for our students to prosper. We boast an overarching commitment to our students, and we will stop at nothing to see them succeed. We solve problems every single day.

Problem-solving begins and ends with Christ. We can present our issues to him, and he promises to provide strength, wisdom, and creativity to find a solution. In the process, we can be grateful for the circumstances, no matter how inconvenient. Our heavenly Father is faithful to weave wisdom and creative solutions into our situation.

Rooted

When the situation appears lacking, trust the Lord with thanksgiving. He promises to reveal a brand-new perspective.

Refreshed

Reflect on a time when you trusted God in less-than-favorable conditions and he provided a solution that gave you a new perspective.

70

Satisfy

For My people have committed two evils: They have abandoned Me, the fountain of living waters, to carve out for themselves cisterns, broken cisterns that do not hold water.

Jeremiah 2:13

Teaching is like walking uphill in the mud with a piano strapped to your back—and this is on a good day.

As humbling as this story is, God instructed me to write it, because somebody needs to read it. I'll do my best to type it just as God is revealing it.

There are hundreds of "helpful" ways to handle stress, the most common and socially acceptable being liquid refreshment. As we leave our classrooms, reflecting on the stress of the day, we are somehow convinced that the "couch pour" will surely wash it all away.

The lie of the Enemy is to satisfy ourselves at the expense of our own well-being.

It's tempting to go home, pour the beverage, grab the phone, and dive in. To scroll and dwell in the lives of others. Or worse, to scroll and play the comparison game. The smoke and mirrors of the online space is a dangerous place to abide, especially with a beverage on board.

I played this game frequently in the fall of 2022. I had left teaching in May, and this was my first August not consumed by going back to school. My entire purpose was in question.

On any given day, I fluctuated between gut-wrenching despair, paralyzing uncertainty, and crippling fear. All before 8:00 a.m. I sat with my phone, scrolling and watching clip after clip as teachers unpacked and prettied up their classrooms. I anxiously waited for evening so I could pour my beverage and wash it all away. It wasn't pretty.

Just keepin' it real.

As the days progressed, ugly patterns formed. Poor sleep and increased anxiety made the smallest infraction rattle my nerves to the breaking point. My sweet husband was the brunt of much of my mood.

Unfortunately, the relief could not disguise the truth. I knew I was pouring into something that was broken and unable to satisfy. Neither my situation nor the way I viewed it could be improved with my current methodology.

A dear friend of mine had recently gone through an alcohol fast. She told me how much better she felt, how well she slept, and how her anxiety had all but vanished. I was intrigued. As afraid as I was of facing my emotional reality, I knew I had to make a change. God uses people to accomplish his purpose, and he delivered her advice at the perfect time.

It wasn't easy. This new strategy meant I had to lean in and feel the pain, the anxiety, and the uncertainty of this new chapter. I also had to accept the fact that I was carving out this cistern all by myself. There was no one else to blame.

As my habits shifted, I discovered I had fresh energy to wake up early and spend time studying God's Word. My peace increased as I read the passages where God tells us his Word is the only thing that can truly satisfy our thirst.

In the coming months, God started directing me to write this book. Responding to him took another eighteen months and several attempts at my new self-care strategy, but as you can see, here we are.

We serve a God who clearly tells us that he is the only satisfaction we need. His Word is the fountain of living water, the only liquid guaranteed to quench our thirst for peace during the storms of life, or in my case, the dry-desert place.

Before we step into a calling far outside of our comfort zone, seeking satisfaction in God's presence, Word, and truth will fortify us for the journey ahead. Fear can cause us to carve out our own cisterns, to abandon this fountain to chase earthly pleasures for temporary relief. If we honestly ask God *why* we are choosing temporary relief over his presence, he will speak to our heart.

Anything created by man is broken because people are broken. If we find ourselves in the cistern-carving business, we are not required to give two weeks' notice. Immediate termination can free us from bondage and return us to the presence of God. He promises to pour out answers in an endless fountain of living water.

Rooted

Choose God first before seeking the things of this world. Only God, the fountain of living waters, can satisfy a thirsty soul.

Refreshed

Reflect on an area of your life where you experienced peace by choosing God over carving your own broken cistern.

71
Shifting Our Gaze

Rid yourself of a deceitful mouth
And keep devious speech far from you.
Let your eyes look directly ahead
And let your gaze be fixed straight in front of you.

Proverbs 4:24–25

My painfully small classroom had been designed for twenty-eight students, but my classes were thirty-five students on average. Add in the jackets, purses, and backpacks, and it was a veritable obstacle course.

I spent a lot of time obsessing over other teachers' classrooms, walking the halls and peeking in to check out the competition's square footage. I began voicing my feelings of injustice to anyone who would listen. The general response from the veteran teachers was, "Do your time. If you're lucky, eventually you may get a bigger room."

"Eventually" was not what I wanted to hear. I devised a detailed plan to actively manipulate the situation. I talked to various administrators, I complained to my department head, and I whined to everyone within earshot.

After almost a month of my campaign, I was sure I would retire in this cramped classroom. If I'm being real here, my issue was that I thought I deserved a bigger classroom. Wasn't my stellar job performance and growing art program enough to kick someone out of their spacious room so I could move in? The ego monster was raging on the warpath of my pride.

One Friday afternoon during my daily pity party, I heard God's still, small voice: *I'm right here. Have I not given you the desires of your heart? You prayed for a job teaching high school, and here you are, living out your dream job every day. Do you think I'm incapable of providing a larger classroom?* Okay, listen. I am all about going to God for healing or comfort for loved ones, but a bigger classroom? All of a sudden I felt silly.

I can still see where I was standing in my tiny classroom space. I closed my eyes, and I said, "Lord, you have undoubtedly given me the desires of my heart. I prayed for almost ten years to be right here in this room. Small though it may be, I am so grateful for every square inch. I will stop looking at what other teachers were blessed with. If this room is where you call me to stay, I will gladly stay right here. I trust you with whatever you choose to provide."

I went home and enjoyed the first peaceful weekend in months.

On Monday morning, my principal walked into my room unannounced. "I think I have a solution to give you a larger room. On Friday afternoon, the teacher in room 316 resigned unexpectedly. Her room is large, and she has a great storage closet. I think it would be perfect for you."

Seriously? I was speechless.

I had expended so much energy trying to manipulate the situation for gain that I had forgotten what God had already done. Once I stopped playing my pitiful game of comparison and fixed my eyes on my blessings, God moved the mountain in less than three days.

We all face challenging professional circumstances from time to time. That's the nice way to say it, anyway. Sometimes we'd rather say, "This situation [insert word that rhymes with trucks]." The challenge may not be a small classroom or a supply shortage. Maybe you're facing mind-bending discipline issues that drain your will to enter your school. Whatever you're up against, fixing your eyes straight ahead keeps the Enemy from winning the comparison game. Your focus on God weakens the Enemy's grip on your emotions. You can fix your eyes straight ahead on Jesus and reflect on his past faithfulness. Even if your situation never changes, your heart posture surely will.

Rooted

Fix your eyes straight ahead on Jesus. His faithfulness is evident in every detail of our lives.

Refreshed

Reflect on a difficult circumstance when you shifted your gaze to God's faithfulness and regained a heart posture of thanksgiving.

72
Student Responsibility

The plans of the heart belong to a person,
But the answer of the tongue is from the Lord.
All the ways of a person are clean in his own sight,
But the Lord examines the motives.
Commit your works to the Lord,
And your plans will be established.

Proverbs 16:1–3

Teenagers are the best people, kind and generous and ready to work at a moment's notice.

If you're reading this and thinking, *What teenagers are you talking about?* allow me to clarify.

All teenagers. I know—it's a bold statement.

Here's the problem. Our expectations are *way* too low. We tend to approach them with a ready-made attitude that they are lazy, selfish, and indifferent to those around them. We also tend to assume that their motives are less than upright.

What if we saw them as God sees us? Designed with purpose and worthy of mature responsibility?

I taught AP Studio Art for the first time in 2011, a class of juniors and seniors. At the end of the year, a local gallery offered to host our student art show free of charge. The owner was willing to give up her wall space (the entire gallery) and subsequent weekend income to host our work. It was imperative for the show go off without a hitch.

I am a huge proponent of responsibility and accountability, especially for students. In an AP class, students are actually enrolled in a freshman-level college course while still in high school.

Part of the deal with our art show was the students had to hang the show—all 132 pieces. We were expecting about four hundred guests, so this was no small feat. They were required to organize and source all the food and schedule setup and cleanup after the reception. My responsibility was to walk around sipping my coffee in the midst of it.

The day before the show, as I enjoyed my coffee, students organized and hung all 132 pieces, covering the gallery walls with a year of dedicated fabulousness. We all went home with that job-well-done feeling. The reception was set for the next day—Friday at 6:00 p.m.

At 10:00 a.m. on Friday morning, I received a call from the gallery owner. Upon arrival she found 90 percent of the artwork on the floor. The gallery had no formal hanging system, and we were experiencing a humid month of May in North Carolina. The hundreds of masking-tape rolls used to hang the artwork had given way overnight. Thankfully, this arresting phone call came in during my AP Studio Art class. I turned to the students (with a giant pit in my stomach) to deliver the bad news.

Without skipping a beat, they put their heads together and devised a plan to go back to the gallery right after school, fresh tape rolls in hand. When the show started at 6:00 p.m., every piece of artwork was safely back on the walls. Mission accomplished. We welcomed more than five hundred guests that evening. Family and friends were there, and the local newspaper even sent a reporter to write a piece highlighting our AP program, complete with a photo spread and student interviews. Best of all, the entire event was curated by the students. I can still see their smiles. It was one of the most beautiful evenings of my career.

Our students are thirsty for responsibility. When we release our grip on a situation, genuinely trusting them to handle it, growth and maturity result. These people are only a few short years away from adult independence. Shifting the focus from us and handing them over to God allows him to show up and work. As we guide these young people toward adulthood, let's remember why we love teaching. We love it because student success is at the core of our being. This job is all about them, and God working through us as we teach. Let's commit every event, every lesson, and every presentation to the Lord and watch him work out his plans in our classrooms.

Rooted

Commit every work in your classroom to the Lord, allowing him to faithfully establish your plans.

Refreshed

Reflect on a situation when you released your grip and allowed God to work through your students to accomplish his plans.

73
Sending a Message

Whatever you do, do your work heartily, as for the Lord and not for people, knowing that it is from the Lord that you will receive the reward of the inheritance. It is the Lord Christ whom you serve.

Colossians 3:23–24

Everything we do sends a message, whether intentional or not. We project an image to the outside world based on our words and actions.

At the beginning of the school year, in each of my classes we established our simple yet focused classroom mission—to be fabulous every single day.

Our first art project, a visual autobiography, was created by assembling various collaged elements that reflected our personalities and interests. Because it was a cut-and-paste endeavor with added line designs, craftsmanship was key to a successful outcome. It was also the largest scoring component of the rubric.

On the first day of the project, I posted a collection of student artwork on my bulletin board from years past. Some of it was quite impressive, some of it not so much. (The names had long since been removed.) Providing an array of possible scoring options was a huge help, especially for students who had never created a visual autobiography before. Seeing examples of what to do and what not to do offered students clear expectations prior to beginning the project.

I opened the project introduction with this thought: "If you didn't know me and I sent you an email with every word misspelled, what would you think?"

Always with slight hesitation, they replied, "We would think you were stupid?"

"Of course you would. All you had to go on is the email. Everything we do in life sends a message. Whether we want it to or not. Your artwork tells a story about you to everyone who views it. It should be beautiful, carefully and deliberately crafted, just like you."

I honestly think some kids have never been told how precious they are. I'd seen some bewildered looks over the years, but this initial conversation with my new students brought more than one set of raised eyebrows.

I didn't need to spend weeks in the classroom to evaluate student potential. Every student was capable of achieving success, no matter the subject. Two things I knew for sure: God created each of them, and his plans for them were good. All that remained was for me to commit myself fully to the task of teaching them how to be the best they could possibly be.

Somewhere along the line, we as teachers came to believe that students prefer learning that's quick and easy. As we bought into the lie, we lowered the bar little by little. I'm not sure if it's a result of the pandemic, social media, or shortened attention spans, but we've lowered our expectations. And shame on us, because nothing is further from the truth.

I'm here to bring you good news. Our students are capable of great things, and they are gifted by God himself to accomplish them. If we believe it, they are more likely to believe it. Let's get down to business and educate them based on their value. As the teacher, we are able to set expectations that bring the bar higher. As a classroom community, we all rejoice together as they exceed it.

God tells us to "do your work heartily, as for the Lord and not for people, knowing that it is from the Lord that you will receive the reward of the inheritance. It is the Lord Christ whom you serve." We don't do it to outperform fellow educators (in person or online), for the likes, for the shares, or for the follows. We do it for the Lord, because he has placed us on a mission field in the form of a classroom.

Rooted

A high bar sends a message of value: "I know you can do this because I know how amazing you are. I also know this even before I get to know you."

Refreshed

Reflect on a class whose mindset was transformed as you set the bar high and rejoiced as they skyrocketed past it.

74
Digging a Firm Foundation

Now why do you call Me, "Lord, Lord," and do not do what I say? Everyone who comes to Me and hears My words and acts on them, I will show you whom he is like: he is like a man building a house, who dug deep and laid a foundation on the rock; and when there was a flood, the river burst against that house and yet it could not shake it, because it had been well built.

Luke 6:46–48

Accountability contributes to success.

Student success hinges on accountability. Theirs and ours.

Let's talk about our classroom spaces and materials for a moment. Anyone else hanging on the frazzled edge over students not respecting either?

This is where accountability comes in clutch.

The classroom is a lifeless space with four walls, until the students arrive. The space takes its first breath when they enter, and it's never the same space twice. The difference from year to year is in the unique makeup of every group. Each class stakes a claim to the space, making it their own. It sounds counter-intuitive to how we perceive our classroom. It's our room, with our name on the door. It's actually not our room at all—it belongs to the district—moreover, the taxpayers. So if it belongs to the taxpayers anyway, aren't those the parents of the students in the room? Technically, I guess the room belongs to the students.

When I explained this to my classes during the first days of school, I got the strangest looks. Students are accustomed to a territorial classroom approach, which unintentionally establishes a "me versus all of you" mindset. "This is my classroom, and you will act a certain way while you are here." Please don't misunderstand me—rules are important, and firm guidelines for positive behavior are necessary, no question.

Early on in my career, when I established our classroom space as a "home away from home," students were more apt to invest in keeping it in order. Taking it a step further, we had contractual obligations on just about every material the students used. It's a bit of work to set up on the front end, but once the accountability is in place, no more supply destruction. No more crusty paint palettes and brushes in the sink. No more broken pencils.

Sounds like Utopia, I know, but it's easily achievable. Wordy expectations said in passing without firmly documented procedures are difficult to enforce and easy to forget. Heck, sometimes I forget what I said (well, most times is more like it). We had a half-page contract for every unit, signed by students and parents. Consequences varied depending on the unit, and each one was vetted through administration first. We all know the value of covering all the angles.

We can start digging the foundation for our classroom community on the first day of school. Verse 48 says that "when there was a flood," not "if" there was a flood. Education will bring torrential downpours to our classrooms. God has given us a simple blueprint for building a strong house to withstand the storm. We need a house built on our actions as we hear God's Word, in addition to classroom procedures and accountability.

We can't just talk about digging a deep foundation—we have to act, just like the man in this passage. He built his house by digging his foundation on the rock of Christ. He walked the walk. As believers we can weather any storm in our classroom knowing our house will not shake. Trials are imminent; we cannot avoid them. We stay safe because we live a life accountable to God. It's a daily dig—going to him, hearing his words, and acting on them. Asking him for direction in our teaching and mentoring daily. Relying on him to answer all issues. If we model our classroom community on our relationship with Christ, we dig a foundation based on his Word. When accompanied by firm procedures, our room will be safe from potential flooding.

Rooted

Building our "classroom house" on the rock of firmly established procedures ensures accountability and protection from the dreaded classroom materials chaos.

Refreshed

Reflect on a time when you laid a strong foundation in your classroom, hearing God's Word and acting on it.

75
Life Chats

So will My word be which goes out of My mouth;
It will not return to Me empty,
Without accomplishing what I desire,
And without succeeding in the purpose for which I sent it.

Isaiah 55:11

Ever heard these questions in your mind?

Does it even matter?

Is anybody listening?

Does anybody even care?

It does matter. They are listening. They do care.

Our students face an onslaught of technical chaos (my new term for social media) every waking second of their day. They don't have the luxury of relying on life experience to filter through it. They haven't been on the planet long enough. I was fond of illustrating this by telling them, "I have shoes older than you."

They do have the benefit of *our* life experiences though. Even better, they have the benefit of our faith.

Teachers have a captive audience for as long as seven hours a day, five days a week. God has a plan and purpose for every person under the sound of our voice. When we choose to send forth words of kindness, godly wisdom, and encouragement, seeds of student success take root. It's not just about learning to draw—it's about learning to navigate life. To lean into difficulty and do hard things.

"Life chats" were a regular occurrence in my room, usually as I stopped by a table to check on work progress—a quick five-minute discourse, prompted by any number of questions or life topics. I kept it short because anything over a few minutes saturated their attention span. Life happens in short clips these days.

We talked frequently about high school being a bubble. It's "One cookie per customer." Failure is not the option it once was. But college? The workforce? Marriage? Success in these areas is a result of individual effort and "intestinal fortitude" (guts). Occasionally I would slip in a carefully worded comment on how a close walk with the Lord had given me the wisdom and strength to make it this far. As I walked away, I asked God to water the seeds.

One year before Christmas break, I had nine former students return to school for a visit. They bounced into my classroom overflowing with tales from their college experiences and fledgling adulthood. Whether they were in school or in the workforce, they couldn't wait to tell me how the life lessons from those five-minute chats in my classroom had resurfaced at just the right time to help guide them. Since they were no longer my students, I asked them if they were attending church. Yep. Right there in the middle of public school. I was talking to the graduates, but there were ears all over the room. I never missed a well-timed opportunity to send out a word of hope. Years later, after countless visits like this, I realized that much of what we had discussed (and how much they had overheard) had taken root. Everything from improved study habits to glorious second chances at a new lease on life. A five-minute chat with a lifetime of return.

God's truths never return void. His Word is alive and powerful, and he uses us to send it out into the world to accomplish his work. God's agenda is for everyone to come to know him and live a joy-filled life in the shelter of his wings. As teachers, we can send out words of God's hope in our classrooms in our daily conversations. We can discuss the joy of the Lord with coworkers, former students, and parents. Our words directed to our students can be kind and encouraging at all times, offering a sense of safety and peace. Chatting with them about their futures is an opportunity to reassure them that there is a plan for their life and help to ease their fears. Although indirect, this is the message of God's love for every student in our care. What a privilege to come alongside them with encouragement for their future, confident that God is accomplishing his plans through us.

Rooted

They are listening. They do care. It does matter. Keep speaking, and ask God to use every word to accomplish his purpose.

Refreshed

Reflect on an occasion when a student (or students) returned for a visit to share the blessing received from your godly wisdom and direction.

76
The Right Shoes

Stand firm therefore, having belted your waist with truth, and having put on the breastplate of righteousness, and having strapped on your feet the preparation of the gospel of peace.

Ephesians 6:14–15

There is no shortage of advice in online teacher forums. And endless supply of information, from how to craft a rubric to where to buy the best pencil sharpener.

The one question that pops up repeatedly is this fan favorite: "What are the best shoes for teaching?" We all have our go-to brands—my personal favorite is Merrell (and I am not a brand affiliate, just a fan).

There is no shortage of human opinions on the best shoes for your human feet. But if we want to survive the marathon called teaching, God has sage advice on the best shoes for the race in Ephesians 6:15.

He tells us to strap on our feet "the preparation of the gospel of peace." This is strong language, commanding us to suit up and get ready—the race is about to start. I find it interesting that we have to prepare by putting our own shoes on. God doesn't do it for us. He provides the shoes, but we have to put them on our feet. The terrain in education is rough. A firm understanding of Christ's gift of salvation, staying close to him, and seeking his wisdom helps us prepare for peace along the way. The preparation of the gospel of peace will steady us as we navigate the rocky terrain.

Can we talk for a moment about the physical demands of working in education? How about the petri dish of germs circling our immune system? We all know it's easier to be sick at school than plan to be absent.

During my student-teaching tenure, I contracted a wicked case of bronchitis. Dosed to the gills on cough medicine and antibiotics, I spent a grueling two weeks teaching drawing, painting, and handbuilding when all I wanted to do was give in, lie down, and sleep. Unfortunately, I couldn't. Our program only allowed for two absences during our student-teaching tenure. I prayed daily for God to fill me with the strength and peace to make it to 3:15 p.m.

Exhaustion (and sickness) threatens our mood, our responses to our students and coworkers, and our thought patterns. The Enemy preys on our low energy, coming at us with spiritual attacks in our weakest moments. When we recognize his advances, we can call on God for peace and strength to resist.

We are called to prepare our hearts and minds with God's gospel of peace. Our relationship with God promises to carry us forward when we feel we have no strength left.

If we're gonna make it in this business, we better learn to prepare. As believers, we can rest in God's faithfulness. He will provide. Our role is to get ready. Nobody is better aware of how to prepare (hey, that rhymes) than educators. Preparation is in our bones. When we put on the shoes that get us ready to experience God's peace in our classrooms, we cannot fail. The gospel of peace is God's good news of his Son, Jesus Christ, who died for all of us. As we copy, cut, laminate, organize, and deliver instruction, our job can feel thankless and tedious. The right shoes stabilize our stance and our walk. The ability to prepare is a blessing worthy of praise. As God prepares us to walk into the routine day after day, we can be confident that we carry with us a message of peace and success. And when we put on the shoes of grace and peace, we stand fully prepared to face anything that comes our way.

Rooted

Outfit your mind and heart with God's gospel of peace—the only shoes capable of helping you navigate the educational terrain ahead.

Refreshed

Reflect on a time when you properly prepared your feet and allowed the gospel of peace to carry you through an exhausting season in the classroom.

77
Trusting God with Our Roster

Listen to advice and accept discipline,
So that you may be wise the rest of your days.
Many plans are in a person's heart,
But the advice of the Lord will stand.

Proverbs 19:20–21

T*he Message* translation says it like this: "We humans keep brainstorming options and plans, but God's purpose prevails."

So who's actually in control?

Not us.

In the beginning of my career, I played a game called Roster Recognizance. Not a real game, but a rather deceptive mind game straight from the Enemy.

It went something like this: In early August, as soon as the system allowed, I logged into the school's website to see who was on my roster for the upcoming school year. I combed over every name, and the anxiety built. I saw students whom other teachers called "difficult." Now remember, it was August. I was supposed to be enjoying my summer. But I was not. Instead, I was headed down the rabbit hole of anxiety and worry, borrowing stress from tomorrow and ruining today.

I emailed and texted other teachers in the department to get "the scoop" on the students whose names I didn't recognize. I heard about how "this student is awesome" and "that student never does anything" and "this kid is a waste" and so on. This feedback only served to heighten my angst. The scenarios formed in my mind, ranging from bad to worse. You get the picture, and maybe you can relate. On several occasions I contacted the guidance counselors, hoping I could manipulate a schedule change before school started. A phone call based solely on the opinions of others. So much for a relaxing August.

With all this student information swimming in my mind, I started the year off building community and telling students *who* they were—amazing people with a distinct purpose, and that purpose was to be fabulous. I also spent a significant amount of time praying that my imagination would take a rest so we could get a strong start to the school year. As the semester progressed, I noticed that all the time I'd spent worrying in August was wasted. Those "difficult" students"? Not my experience at all. Not only were they not difficult, they were thriving.

The verse above begins with us listening to advice. Oh, I had listened to plenty of advice—it just wasn't from the right source. Instead of waiting until school started and committing the school year to the Lord, I allowed my coworkers to tell me who my students were and how they would act in my classroom. Fear is a spiritual ploy of the Enemy. His plan was to convince me how awful the school year would be with these students in my classroom. The fear robbed me of the remainder of my summer and took my joy along with it. And I did it to myself.

Every human relationship is exclusive to the two people in it. The teacher-student relationship is no different. This is where God comes in. When we approach all students as God sees them, full of potential and purpose, they feel empowered to succeed in our classrooms. Their former reputation is in the past, a situation for another person's classroom. In our class, we have a chance to change the narrative, shifting the way these "difficult" students see themselves. Make no mistake—they are fully aware of their "reputation." Heeding God's advice gives us the wisdom to extend a fresh outpouring of God's love to every student on our roster, especially the "difficult" ones.

The takeaway? Relax and enjoy the summer. Log in to the system when you return to school. The students on your roster have been placed there by God for a purpose. You can get excited about who God has placed in your classes, knowing the class makeup is his design. When we choose to see our classroom as a room full of divine appointments, the best is yet to come.

Rooted

Listen and act on God's timely wisdom. Trust him to fill your roster with divine appointments.

Refreshed

Reflect on a time when you ignored the opinions of others and trusted God to build your roster.

78
Reframing Community

So, as those who have been chosen of God, holy and beloved, put on a heart of compassion, kindness, humility, gentleness, and patience; bearing with one another, and forgiving each other, whoever has a complaint against anyone; just as the Lord forgave you, so must you do also.

Colossians 3:12–13

What makes a successful classroom community?

Rules? Expectations? Both?

We are often consumed by the multitude of strategies that build a classroom community, desperate for the perfect solution to our lack-of-student-engagement woes.

Maybe it's easier than it seems.

I can't help but think of that invisible wall between us and the students. It starts with our name on the door and extends to that sacred space we call our teacher desk. This is *my* classroom, *my* name on the door. I need you to stand back from *my* desk—you're too close. And let's not forget the pandemic, when we cordoned off our desks with colored tape on the floor to keep students six feet away. No wonder everyone was on edge. Those were scary times.

Now that we're on the other side of the lockdown, facing rampant apathy and minute attention spans, how do we reframe the narrative? How do we create a close-knit and productive community of learners?

Will the class be "our class" or "me implementing a system of rules so you will behave a certain way"? Please don't misunderstand. I am not at all implying that rules and classroom-management strategies are not necessary. Rock-solid classroom procedures and management skills are single-handedly the most important piece of the teaching puzzle. Without them we invite mutiny and chaos.

At the end of my second year of teaching, I was moved to a larger classroom. During the move, I misplaced my handy-dandy School Rules poster. When I set up my new space, it was mysteriously gone, either by mistake or on purpose. Knowing me, it was on purpose. I'm a bit of a rebel. A list of rules on the wall seemed like an invitation for high school shenanigans. My next-door teacher neighbor had a list of words that were not allowed to be uttered in her classroom. How effective do you think that was? Yeah, not very. That list grew from a dozen words to almost a hundred by Thanksgiving break, some of them creative indeed.

What if our first-day-of-school speech started with, "Today I want to focus only on getting to know each of you, because this class is about your success. You are the most important people in this room." Imagine the bewildered looks and the questions that would follow. I've seen these looks firsthand, and they always make me smile.

"But what about the rules? Where's the syllabus? How many bathroom passes do we get?"

"We'll get to all of that eventually." (We actually don't get to it for more than a week, but that's a devotion for another time.) "Right now I want us to focus on our success as a group. We are chosen to be fabulous."

"But you don't even know us."

"Not right now, no. But it will be my privilege to get to know you. Each one of you has been called into this room for a purpose. You think you got stuck in here, but you didn't. You have been hand selected to sit right here at this exact time. My hope for you is that every day this will be the class you can't wait to get to and the class you can't stand to leave."

These verses give us simple, actionable steps to build a strong, supportive community in our classrooms. As God's children, we are chosen and capable of exhibiting these qualities, each one of them completely free to enact. Kindness, humility, gentleness, and patience, delivered with a heart of compassion for the young souls in our care. A roomful of forgiveness between all of us regardless of the complaint. These attributes are a complete description of how the Lord approaches us. What a beautiful picture of a classroom environment. In these fruitful conditions, a foundation of trust develops. Anxiety dissipates. A classroom vibe of peaceful productivity is born.

Rooted

A successful classroom community mirrors God's approach toward his children—steeped in kindness, humility, gentleness, and patience, delivered with a heart of compassion and overflowing with forgiveness.

Refreshed

Reflect on the beginning of the school year and all the ways you exhibit God's love as you build your classroom community.

79
Waiting and Seeking

The Lord is good to those who await Him,
To the person who seeks Him.

Lamentations 3:25

Picture it. December 2008. The ink on the teaching license was not yet dry.

The housing market was in free fall. Due to cuts in funding, the potential teaching position where I did my practicum was not approved by the board. I was heartbroken. I had spent three months planning every nuance of my dream classroom. It had been so close to becoming a reality.

Student loan payments began in July 2009.

In early January I was out walking the neighborhood, fantasizing about the dream classroom that would remain a permanent dream. I ran into my neighbor, who told me she was the coordinator for substitute teachers for our local intermediate school. (This was back before automated sub-calling systems.) She asked me how much I wanted to work.

"Every day of the week. Any grade, any class," I said.

If you have never worked as a substitute teacher, let me paint you a mental picture. It's like that show *Let's Make a Deal*. What you'll find behind the mystery door is a trial-by-fire course in classroom management with a consolation prize of $68 dollars a day. Buckle up.

I was convinced I would be heading into my own art classroom in the fall of 2009, filled with wonderful students and beautiful artwork, living the dream I had been imagining since 2001. Instead, I was opening the mystery door every day and combing district websites within a fifty-miles radius for job openings in the middle of a disastrous economic downturn. It was terrifying.

I had been praying for God's direction since the start of this journey, and I knew he had me in this holding pattern for a reason. I decided to give each day my best no matter what was behind the door. I approached each class as if they were my own—my dream classroom. I spent time talking with the students in each class, asking them what they enjoyed about school and what they wished were different. I received a wealth of professional development with every class I covered.

I became a familiar face among the kids. When I walked in each day, the kids waiting in the lobby would yell, "Who are you subbing for, Mrs. Fox?" If it was their teacher, they would shout, "YESSSSS!" Major confidence boost.

I began to see that those days had significant purpose. I arrived at school each day asking God to show me who I needed to encourage, how to engage with each student effectively, and how best to learn from them. He helped me see the opportunities and divine appointments in each classroom and not waste time dreaming of a classroom that didn't exist . . . yet.

That season playing *Substitute Teacher Let's Make a Deal* ended up being one of no deals at all. It slowly became a season of complete trust. Don't get me wrong—I still dreamed of my future high school art classroom. But instead of wasting time in self-pity, I fully immersed myself in my substitute-teacher season. God's goodness came in the form of invaluable on-the-job training. More training than I ever received in any college classroom.

Waiting is a difficult task. Our minds can easily become the Enemy's playground, with thoughts of *what if* and *why not* stealing our joy. God keeps 100 percent of his promises, and his promise here is that he is good to those who wait on him to act, to the person who seeks him.

Waiting and seeking seem like two opposite concepts. Waiting feels like doing nothing. Seeking feels like action, as if we are attempting to obtain something. We can wait on the Lord while we seek his presence in our hearts. When we are still, spending time with him and fully trusting his plan, these are our times of greatest peace. Seeking his will for our perfect placement, trusting that he knows what is best. God's promised response to our waiting and seeking is his goodness, and his goodness never fails.

I knew that God would reveal my dream classroom in his perfect timing. I wasn't there yet. I was in my substitute-teacher season, and my priority there was walking thirty squirrely eight year olds to the lunchroom on time without losing anyone.

Rooted

There is a wealth of information in a season of waiting. Seek God as you wait—there is much to learn.

Refreshed

Reflect on a time when you saw the goodness of the Lord as you waited on him and sought his presence.

80

Know Your Strengths

Lord, You have searched me and known me. You know when I sit down and when I get up; You understand my thought from far away. You scrutinize my path and my lying down, and are acquainted with all my ways. Even before there is a word on my tongue, behold, Lord, You know it all.

Psalm 139:1–4

Wherever you are today, please know this. God is not at all surprised by your situation.

He is fully aware of every minute detail.

As God's children, we can be certain of these three things.

1. He knows us.
2. He understands us.
3. He watches over us.

Here's a thought. What if we approached our students the same way God approaches us? With a desire to know them, understand them, and watch over them. It's much easier to care for people whom you know and understand. When we are familiar with our students and understand their personalities and circumstances, a classroom community is born.

What if getting to know them is our number one priority on day one? Meeting them where they are, ready to understand their situation apart from our classroom rules or course content. A first day of school free of a syllabus overview and a list of rules. Not one word about grading policies or bathroom passes. Whoa.

A young lady named Lauren graced my drawing roster back in 2018. In the early days of the semester, she and several other students revealed their obsession with keeping things in order. You don't know this about me, but I'll admit it now. I do not share this quality. As an art teacher, a lack of organization develops quickly into classroom chaos. Boxes and bins of materials overflowing with mismatched art supplies all over the room. We've all seen the magazines stacked up and sliding off the counter, their scraps multiplying before our eyes. It's a scene.

During the Get to Know You project (our first project of the school year), Lauren revealed that she enjoyed cleaning and organizing, no matter the space or items. During the project, she discovered several other students who shared her love for organization. Not only were Lauren and her new friends huge fans of order, but they were frequently early finishers, completing lessons a day or two before their classmates. Knowing they had a knack for organizing, I put them to work. By the second week of September, the entire classroom was in order. I've never seen students so thrilled to clean and organize a space. They even designed a labeling system that remained in place from that class onward. My stress was drastically reduced, and their joy in helping was obvious.

Just as God knows us, he also knows each one of our students. He created each of them with specific gifts, and through them he offers us a roomful of assistance, with each person having a gift to contribute to the group. With thirty-plus people in the room, many hands make light work. We are not meant to go it alone. God gives us a fresh community of helpers with every roster. The classroom mindset is not "us against them." It's "all of us in it together, invested in the process and headed for success."

Whether we believe this or not, students love to help. Helping others is God's dopamine—it genuinely makes us feel good. When we see them as God sees them—capable of playing a role in our classroom community—and welcome their contribution, our attitude is God focused, not us focused. As we get to know them, we have the privilege of discovering their strengths. When we make time to help students discover their strengths, a productive classroom environment awaits.

Rooted

God has provided us with a classroom full of helpers, each one gifted in their own way. Tap into their strengths and praise their contributions. All the help we need is right in front of us.

Refreshed

Reflect on a time when you invited students to use their strengths in your classroom and the result was a smooth and productive learning experience.

81

Expect the Best

The Lord is my strength and my shield; my heart trusts in him, and he helps me. My heart leaps for joy, and with my song I praise him.

Psalm 28:7 NIV

As noted earlier, I worked as a substitute teacher for six months prior to teaching full-time.

Some of it was at the middle school level.

Subbing middle school is a lot like dropping a raw T-bone into a tank full of sharks. I was the T-bone.

This was my only teaching option until I could secure a full-time position, hopefully in the fall. If you've ever experienced the life of a substitute teacher, you can relate. A trial-by-fire—95 percent classroom management and 5 percent actual teaching. I considered myself fairly adept at controlling behaviors—the problem is, you never know what you're walking into. It's this inconsistency that brings anxiety.

With no other choice, off I went, fear and all. *What fresh hell awaits, and how fast can 3:15 get here?*—my initial attitude before I set foot in the classroom. This mindset of assuming the worst was wearing me out, and fast.

If I was to sustain an entire semester of this, I needed to get my head on straight.

It took some time, but I changed my approach from fearing the unknown to releasing my day to God before I walked into the school. I used the rearview-mirror method and reflected on all he had done in the months before. He had faithfully sustained me during my last months of student teaching. I'd taught every day with the worst case of bronchitis imaginable and without missing a single day. How I had forgotten this in the short weeks since graduation was beyond me.

My daily request was simple. "Holy Spirit, fill me up and equip me with your wisdom so every student sees you in me."

Shortly after I began praying that prayer, I was scheduled to cover for a seventh-grade social studies teacher. Once the attendance sheet was completed, I asked a young man named Chad to deliver the paperwork to the attendance secretary. I had never subbed in this class before, but it was apparent that Chad was a discipline issue. (It might have been the way he entered the room jumping over the first desk and screaming, "Yesssss! A sub!"*)* Nevertheless, I approached him with the attendance paper in hand.

"Sir, would you do me a favor? I need a responsible student to deliver the attendance to the front office. Would you be so kind as to do this for me?" His look of bewilderment spoke volumes. Chad was clearly convinced nobody trusted him—hence the note from the teacher to not allow him out of my sight.

As Chad left the room, attendance paper in hand, one of the other kids said, "You know he's not coming back."

Not only did he return, but he ended up organizing the colored-pencil sets and cleaning the whiteboard, with a smile on his face the whole time. It was a good day to be a substitute teacher, with many more good days to follow.

Once I began offering God each new class of temporary students, everything changed. Did the middle schoolers get less rambunctious? Of course not. They're tweens. It's the Wild West on the best of days. What changed was how I approached them, fully trusting God to strengthen and shield all of us, to help us in all aspects of our school day. It was a blessing to be their substitute teacher. Our time together was a divine appointment full of learning potential for all of us, not something to be endured.

Why we gravitate toward the worst-possible scenario always baffles me. Assuming the worst in the face of God's promises seems ridiculous, especially in light of who he is—the creator of the universe. I fell into that trap too. But he is our strength and our shield, the one in whom we trust, our constant source of help. This strength and protection build a trust that prompts us to ask our heavenly Father for help in any situation. No wonder the psalmist's heart leaped for joy! No matter our teaching season, temporary or permanent, our hearts can overflow with songs of praise, knowing we can trust a God whose ability to strengthen and shield us knows no limits.

Rooted

Trust God to provide you with all the strength and protection needed to trust him fully in your current teaching season.

Refreshed

Reflect on a time when you trusted God to strengthen and protect you in a teaching season of fear or uncertainty.

82
Waiting with Strength & Courage

Wait for the Lord;
Be strong and let your heart take courage;
Yes, wait for the Lord.

Psalm 27:14

Waiting patiently on the Lord takes practice.

God knows that my patience needs refining, and he is masterfully adept at time-frame management—his time frame, not mine.

During my student teaching in the fall of 2008, I had the privilege of working alongside Jess, a creative and talented art teacher in her first year with the school district. We became fast friends, and she provided words of professional wisdom and guidance that I still utilize today.

The tanking economy resulted in Jess's teaching position being eliminated for the 2009–2010 school year. I was about to graduate in December without any job prospects. We were both in need of a job. We submitted applications to every school district within a fifty-mile radius. In the summer of 2009, jobs were scarce.

I had passed on an offer for an elementary school position in June. As much as I knew passing was the right thing to do, the Enemy's accusing voice kept the fear simmering: *You* had *a job in the palm of your hand, and you gave it away. Stupid.*

As the summer passed, I spent almost every spare moment checking the district websites for potential job openings. Each day was the same—log on, scroll down, and see . . . nothing. As August 1 arrived, nervousness set in. I had just made my first student loan payment—only 119 more payments remaining.

Then came August 11. I walked into my kitchen, popped open my laptop, and immediately felt the Lord guiding me: *You need to look at the ISS website.* Iredell-Statesville Schools was our neighboring district—I had been checking their site daily for weeks. "Yeah, sure, I'll check." School started in two weeks. I wasn't hopeful.

And there it was. If I close my eyes, I can still see the words on the screen: "Opening: Art Teacher—High School. Lake Norman High School." Seven miles from my house. Excitement took over as I read the job listing. As thrilled as I was, a still, small voice in my mind quietly spoke up: *You need to tell Jess about the job opening.*

What? I already gave away one job!

Jess was a fellow teacher (also out of a job) who had four years' experience and advanced-level certification, not to mention an amazing portfolio of student artwork. I had nothing but a fresh teaching license. So I did what anyone desperately needing a job would do—I called Jess and told her about the job opening. With every word that left my mouth, I could hear the nagging voice of the Enemy all over again telling me how stupid I was.

The next morning I drove those seven short miles and walked into the front office of the school, résumé in hand. A gentleman lounged behind the counter with his feet up. I had no idea he was the principal, covering the front desk while the office personnel were out.

"I'm here to inquire about the art teacher position." *And sometime later today, my way-better-qualified friend will also be here to inquire.*

His response was nothing short of miraculous. "Really? Well, as of this morning, I need to hire *two* art teachers."

Another art teacher had resigned unexpectedly that morning. Wow. Talk about God's time-frame management.

Fast-forward. Jess and I spent two wonderful years teaching together before her husband was transferred out of state. Looking back, I saw God's hand in the entire situation, for both of us.

Don't let the Enemy make you feel stupid as you wait on the Lord—the Adversary has no power over us unless we give in to his lies. As believers we can be fully confident in God's plans—they are always better than our own. We can also rest in his ability to bring opportunity at the perfect time. A strong and courageous heart honors the Lord and resists the Enemy.

I was in bad need of some strength and courage during the summer of 2009, and the Lord provided both in a season of waiting. You may be in a waiting season yourself. Maybe you've passed on a sure thing knowing God has something better, but you have no idea what it is. The whole situation may look crazy to you and everyone around you. The Lord is a pro at time-frame management. Be strong and courageous, and wait.

Rooted

Wait on the Lord with strength and confidence. He is an expert in time-frame management.

Refreshed

Reflect on a time when you trusted the Lord and passed on a seemingly perfect opportunity, only to find that his plans far exceeded your own.

83
Taste and See

Taste and see that the Lord is good;
How blessed is the man who takes refuge in Him!

Psalm 34:8

I couldn't taste or see anything good about the year 2020.

We left for spring break on March 7, and it was more than a year before we returned to school.

My entire identity was being a high school teacher. I was completely lost.

When the lockdown came, there I was in my house, separated from my calling, trying to discern what God had for me in that season. He began to nudge me: *I want you to write a devotional book for teachers.*

Okay, Lord. Listen. Lessons I can write. With full confidence. A devotional? Not so much.

The more time I spent praying over this directive, the louder it got, and the more frightened I became. Who am I to write a book? I might be a teacher, but I was certainly no writer. I couldn't help but think of Moses arguing with God about how he was "slow of speech." Boy, could I relate!

I jotted down scattered ideas about the book, all the while reminding God that I was not equipped.

Looking back, I can't help but chuckle. There I was, jotting down ideas that came straight from the experiences God had provided when he'd brought me to the classroom in the first place. He had been equipping me for years, and now he was offering me a chance to slow down and remember. I had no idea where this was going, but I followed anyway.

As the ideas formed, I began to see God's goodness in the lockdown. It was so quiet there. No students, no hustle, no hamster wheel of stress. When the students were no longer there, he remained present and faithful, and I could hear his still, small voice calling me to remember the joy in the job. To recall everything he had done. I was able to taste and see his goodness in this otherwise lonely time.

The writing didn't begin until 2023. It took almost three years and some serious life changes to get me to this point. It was 2022 when I left the classroom and we moved to another state to be near my daughter and her family. It was the hardest thing I ever did.

Remember, I'm a high school art teacher. That's who I am, and it's all that I am.

Is it?

Evidently not, because you're reading this. His message began with your story.

He said, *Teachers are hurting now more than ever. They need to know that I love them, I called them, and I placed every student in their care for a specific purpose. Tell them who I am and how I am already in the classroom, waiting to help. All they need to do is ask.*

So here we are. Me walking in blind obedience as I write, and you reading a book I was sure would never come to exist. A season of isolation allowed me to taste and see God's goodness and experience his presence in an unexpected calling.

Maybe you're in your classroom right now, surrounded by the hustle and laughter of God's children, and the bell is about to ring. Wherever you are, take refuge in the Lord. He is right there with you.

We can use all five senses to align with his presence. This verse tells us specifically to taste and see that the Lord is good. We are to personally experience the goodness of God. This active engagement is a heart posture that guides our teaching practice.

As Jesus followers, the Lord is at the center of how we create community, how we interact with the students, and how we cultivate an atmosphere of safety. It's not merely head knowledge—we actively embody the character of God in our classrooms as teachers after his own heart. Godly character produces an overflow of blessings poured out on our students.

Rooted

Align with the Lord; taste and see how blessed you are to experience his goodness in your classroom.

Refreshed

Reflect on a time when you experienced God's undeniable goodness and his blessings in your classroom.

84
Unexpected Effects of Kindness

Do not let kindness and truth leave you;
Bind them around your neck,
Write them on the tablet of your heart.

Proverbs 3:3

May of 2022 was the last student art show of my teaching career. We had the privilege of showing at a local art gallery—Four Corners Framing and Gallery in downtown Mooresville, North Carolina. If you're ever in town, stop and say hi to Kim—she's the owner, and her dedication to her community and the success of young people is unmatched.

The night of the show, a man I did not know approached me with a story. He had seen the press release of our student show on social media, and he wanted to come and thank me in person. For what, I had no idea.

In the spring of 2010 (my first year teaching), his daughter was a senior in my drawing class. He had moved her to North Carolina from Ohio in December after his divorce, smack in the middle of her senior year. The divorce and the move had left her emotionally broken and fragile. He was afraid she may not graduate. To his relief, she willingly attended school, and after a few weeks was enjoying her new surroundings. Evidently her time in my classroom was a contributing factor in her motivation to graduate amid her pain. He wanted to make sure I knew the impact I had on her life.

I wish I could tell you that I remembered his daughter. There was no aha moment when I recalled her love of my class. That had been my first year in the classroom, and quite honestly, I spent that entire year in survival mode. The only conscious commitment I can remember was one I made to myself. To approach my students with kindness and welcoming grace—this would be the core of my teaching style. These young people (including this man's daughter) were a gift straight from the Lord; I was intently serious about the mark I left on their lives.

When this man revealed to me how tenuous and fragile her situation had been, I was speechless. As a parent, he must have been frantic with worry. There I was, going about my day bouncing around on the countertop (as mentioned earlier, I taught from the countertop a lot in that small room) and teaching drawing skills like they were the greatest thing since sliced bread. I never stopped to consider that some of the people in my classes were suffering terrible loss.

During my survival antics, there in front of me sat this man's daughter, also just trying to survive. In the depths of her sadness, she returned to school each day based, in part, on her experience in my classroom. Maybe it was the countertop teaching. It was pretty lit.

There are no mistakes in life, only divine appointments. Each student is carefully placed in our classrooms on purpose—God's purpose. Our job is to wear kindness and truth around our necks like a medal of honor. To write these attributes on the tablet of our heart—the core of our being. Now there's an educational reference if I ever saw one.

God knows the struggles and needs of every student in our classrooms. He carries their burdens and fights their battles daily. Part of his plan is placing these young people in our care, to witness his love in action. When we lead with kindness and truth, our students receive a blessing, and we may never know its impact. We don't need to know. Our call is to wear these attributes like the champions of success we already are. We are teachers.

This man came to my art show to remind me that kindness does not go unnoticed. God is always working through us in someone's heart.

Rooted

The binding of kindness and truth is our part—the rest is God's part.

Reflect on a time when you found out after the fact the impact of your kindness in the classroom.

85
Comfort in the Valley

Even though I walk through the valley of the shadow of death,
I fear no evil, for You are with me;
Your rod and Your staff, they comfort me.

Psalm 23:4

There are two constants in life.

First, we all find ourselves in a valley from time to time.

Second, no matter where we are, God is always with us.

Education is full of valleys. I could list a few, but you already have one (or more) in mind.

Maybe you're deep in a valley now, wondering if you'll ever find your way out.

Regardless of how vast or deep the valley is, I have good news. God is with us. His presence is unchanging. The better news is that he wants the very best for us.

God's role in the valley is one of comforter. The rod and staff are references to being shepherded, like sheep. Our Good Shepherd guides us through the valley, offering protection from evil. If we allow him to lead, we emerge safely on the other side.

I used to picture this as protection from outside forces. I now see them as the forces in my mind—fear, pride, bitterness—beckoning me to abandon the leading of the One who made me and go it alone for comfort and stability.

Pride is always in the shadows, whispering to me that I know better and can achieve my goals more quickly on my own. I struggled with this during my eight-month season between graduation and landing my first teaching job. It was 2008, and in case that's not resonating, the country was in the middle of a cavernous recession—and my student loan payments were coming due July 1.

In June a teacher friend of mine told me that the art teacher at her school was leaving—the school was one mile from my house. On my friend's recommendation, the job was presented to me on a silver platter. No questions, no interview, no fuss, no muss. Elementary level with a move-in ready classroom. I met the principal and saw my would-be classroom, complete with adorable cubbies and endless art supplies. I could have started unstacking the tiny chairs and organizing the crayons that afternoon. As perfect as it seemed, something was off; I could sense it. As I presented the situation to God, nothing about the job felt right. I also felt him telling me to wait.

So I did what any other person needing to pay off her student loans would do.

I picked up the phone and called a friend of mine whose husband had recently lost his job. She had also graduated from our teaching program with her K-12 certification. Her expertise was elementary school. As I watched the opportunity pass, it felt good to know that my friend would be able to help support her family while living out her dream job. Eighteen years later, she is still teaching at the school.

As everyone around me (including my husband) told me I was nuts, I remained confident of God's guidance in any financial valley. He had not forsaken me yet, and he wasn't about to start now.

We can reach for all sorts of earthly comfort in the valley—hasty decision-making, substance, isolation, gossip, or venting through a keyboard attack on social media. All of these choices provide a temporary feeling of relief. Some of them can plunge us into deeper valleys, only to find ourselves regretful, exhausted, and sad—and still in the valley.

As you read this, where do you see yourself today? Emerging from the ashes like a phoenix? Careening down the rocky hillside? Our location is not unknown to God. He also knows exactly where we are, what we need, and when we need it. In this business called education, teachers traverse the deepest of valleys. That valley leading up to being hired is as deep as it gets, especially when there are bills to pay.

As believers, we claim a peace like no other, knowing that God is with us in every valley. He has designed us and equipped us for a specific purpose. If we trust his leading and wait on his goodness, he is faithful to guide us through with safety and comfort.

Rooted

No matter the valley, allow him to lead. His faithfulness is our assurance that he knows what's best for us.

Refreshed

Reflect on a time when God led you through a deep and challenging valley, with his guiding hand providing answers along the way.

86
Eat Your Own Bread

Now we command and exhort such persons in the Lord Jesus Christ to work peacefully and eat their own bread. But as for you, brothers and sisters, do not grow weary of doing good.

2 Thessalonians 3:12–13

"You're so lucky. You only work eight to three."

Anybody else want to slap this person into next year—or is it just me?

In the beginning of my career, I spent every evening at school until at least 7:00 p.m. and most weekends, designing curriculum, grading work, and attempting to keep my classroom from disappearing in a pile of papers. This schedule had me running on fumes most days.

Sometimes we work alongside people who do not share our same work ethic. If we're not careful, exhaustion can lead to animosity as we watch them arrive at school two minutes before the tardy bell and leave campus as soon as the school day ends.

Some days my tank was so empty that I could barely function, the hair on my neck bristling as the classroom next door went dark at 3:15 p.m. On those days I took a little extra time and surrendered the animosity to the One who made the day. He graciously allowed me to wake up and face whatever lay ahead. When it seemed like the day would never end, he never failed to remind me to direct my energy into my own space and not anyone else's.

Our classroom was a home away from home. A place for creativity and hard work, but also a place to feel safe. It was well known that my students (and their friends) were always welcome. During the early years, everyone knew that Mrs. Fox would be there before and after school.

There was a continual display of in-progress and finished artwork on my classroom whiteboard and walls. It was a constantly changing and stunning gallery, corner-to-corner evidence of hard work. These walls were a genuine source of pride for my students. Sometimes they stopped in and brought visitors for a quick gallery tour. Even though I was buried in work and it was after school hours, the exchange always brought a smile, "Dude, you gotta see this" and "Whoa! That is sooooo good!"

As I've mentioned, the current class pictures hung on the whiteboard, and the past class photos covered my storage cabinet— a sea of smiling faces welcoming our visitors.

After the gallery tour, students combed the class pictures looking for people they might know, friends and siblings, past and present students. It was like a game of Where's Waldo. This was a place of belonging, and they saw a legacy in those photos that would live on forever on my cabinet doors.

I don't know what the hook is in your classroom. There is a reason students can't wait to get to school and enter your safe and welcoming community. Maybe it's obvious how much you care. Maybe your room is free of unkind words and bigotry. Whatever the reason, managing the duties of teaching and actively caring for our students is both mentally and physically draining.

We are commanded in this passage to work, eat our own bread, and not grow weary of doing good. The temptation to complain about the uneven distribution of the department workload is real. People, we all know that the workload is mammoth. We also know the frustration of an uneven distribution. Satan wants to sow division; God wants our eyes on him and his purpose for us, not on anyone else.

There will always be someone who's not pulling their weight. Instead of focusing on their lacking contribution, let's eat the bread in our own classrooms, unaffected by anything outside our four walls. We have the privilege of pouring his grace and mercy into our students' lives—even if it is exhausting.

God has gifted us with a room full of people to work hard for, and our efforts will not return void.

Rooted

Regardless of how rested our classroom neighbor may be, God has a command for us—we are to eat our own bread, work hard, and not grow weary.

Refreshed

Reflect on a time when your energies needed redirected back into your own classroom space and purpose.

87
Hard Work

Go to the ant, you lazy one,
Observe its ways and be wise,
Which, having no chief,
Officer, or ruler,
Prepares its food in the summer
And gathers its provision in the harvest.

Proverbs 6:6–8

"Don't waste time. You never get it back."

Life is both fragile and fast.

It's not surprising that this truth is difficult for teens to understand.

They haven't been on the planet that long. Life choices and the trajectory of their consequences are still unseen. Helping them understand the value of time and the importance of their work ethic is a daily challenge for any educator.

"We need to develop a rock-solid work ethic that transcends every task set before us. Your work is an extension of *you*. It is evidence of who you are and the effort you put forth."

I expected a *lot* from my students. With no expectations, little is achieved—or received. I saw every student in the room as Jesus sees them. Full of potential, gifted for a purpose, and there for a reason. Each person is a divine appointment, and everyone is capable of creating amazing work. Once the mission and the mindset are in place, the sky's the limit.

Excellence was the cornerstone of our classroom mission. Everything we did, we accomplished with an attitude of excellence, because that is who God created us to be. This was our mindset. There was no room for anything less.

In 2011 I had a student named Rachel who possessed a propensity for perfection in everything she created. She wasted no time, no matter the task. I was constantly telling her that her hard work and her dedication to excellence were evident to everyone. Whether she was drawing or painting, she worked tirelessly, so much so that she graduated a semester early. I knew she would go on to do great things.

That was almost fifteen years ago. I recently received a note from Rachel via Facebook. I had not talked with her since graduation. She told me that today she enjoys a career as a millwright. I must confess I had to look it up. Millwrights install, maintain, diagnose, and repair industrial machines that usually cost millions of dollars. This work requires precision welding techniques to set machinery within a thousandth of an inch.

"Mrs. Fox, we do a *lot* of welding, and I never knew anything about it until I tried it and instantly related it to drawing! So needless to say, I'm a welder now haha. But my time and patience and creative ideas come from your influence."

In this passage we see the tiny ant working patiently to prepare for the harvest to come. He works all summer, when it would be more fun to play. Nobody tells him to work. He is created by God to work instinctively. If God gives this tiny creature time and patience to carry his food to safe storage, how much more will he provide us with time and patience to help our students understand their own value through hard work?

It's difficult to exercise patience in the classroom, with deadlines all around us. There are due dates and grade reports and graduation requirements. In the midst of this, let's patiently remember that our classes are a sea of God's children preparing for the coming harvest. Whatever our chosen strategies, we can set expectations of excellence in our classrooms. What a privilege to help our students develop their lifelong work ethic.

Rachel said it best. Time and patience are invaluable. Without time we can do nothing. Without patience we work precariously. Learning to use both helps our students cultivate a strong work ethic that prepares them for the coming season of adulthood.

Rooted

Utilize God's gifts of time and patience to guide your students in developing a work ethic with a rich harvest in the next season.

Refreshed

Reflect on a student whose work ethic and self-esteem grew exponentially as you showed them the intrinsic value of hard work.

88
Hospitality

Do not neglect hospitality to strangers, for by this some have entertained angels without knowing it.

Hebrews 13:2

I always viewed my classroom as my second home. A place to welcome strangers and show them their endless potential.

On the first day of school I wrote "WELCOME!!!" in big 3-D letters on my board. Below that, "Prepare to Be Fabulous!" I meant every word. I told them I would eat, sleep, and breathe their fabulousness—150 percent.

Each new day began with me thanking them for coming to school. When students returned from being absent, I greeted them with a boisterous welcome. "Joseph! Where *were* you yesterday?! We missed you!"

Sometimes the answer was, "Oh, I slept in" or "I just stayed home."

My response to this honesty was, "Joseph, have you ever made plans with someone to do something fun and they canceled at the last minute or just didn't show up? That's how I feel when you don't come to my class by choice." This response always got the strangest looks. But I meant it.

At the end of Covid-19, we returned to school on a hybrid schedule. Three days a week in person. I welcomed them with my usual unbridled enthusiasm, and the giant-sized "WELCOME!!!" on the whiteboard. It was such a gift to have students physically present again.

I once had a senior with spotty attendance. It was spring semester, and his senior year had been decimated by the pandemic. No prom, no senior trip, no in-person graduation. It was a difficult time for all of us, but especially the seniors. This young man didn't need my class to graduate. It was a wonder he showed up at all.

As the days progressed, our hybrid class enjoyed some productive discussions about our experiences during lockdown. Specifically, we talked about unexpected blessings. This young man told us how he and his friends spent a lot of time together fishing during lockdown. Sitting on the dock, talking and laughing, trying to catch a bit of normalcy (and maybe a fish) during this otherwise lonely time. These fishing meetups never would have happened if it weren't for the quarantine. He confessed to getting to know people he never would have talked to prior to this and how grateful he was for the friendships.

At the risk of losing my job, I carefully expressed the need for all of us to examine life's lemons and get busy making lemonade. We do not know what the day (or season) will bring, but we can be sure there is a reason. We can also be sure that the reason has a purpose. In this case a group of young people spent quality time together, developing unexpected friendships and navigating a lonely season with one another.

Toward the end of the semester, I noticed this senior's attendance improving and his effort increasing dramatically. One day I was helping him with his portrait drawing, and out of the blue he said, "You know, Mrs. Fox, I only have to come to school in person for your class and English. Most of the time I leave after your class to go fishing."

While this verse speaks to angels, I think we would all agree that our students are angels in God's eyes. Somebody else's children entrusted to our care. If we extend hospitality toward them that is fit for angels, how can they not feel welcome in our classrooms?

Providing a safe, nonjudgmental environment affords a space for open and honest reflection. For our students, this is the purest form of hospitality we can offer. These young people need our support apart from academics. God wants us to offer hospitality fit for an angel sent from heaven. When we open our classrooms to thirty-plus angels, we can be sure God is smiling at our welcome.

Rooted

The Lord loves a genuinely welcoming atmosphere that provides a safe and motivating space for his thirty-plus angels.

Refreshed

Reflect on a student (or students) who responded to the hospitality in your welcoming classroom with improved effort.

89

When Things Go Wrong

Consider it all joy, my brothers and sisters, when you encounter various trials, knowing that the testing of your faith produces endurance.

James 1:2–3

"I love it when things go wrong."

One of my favorite Foxisms, it garnered the most bizarre looks from students.

Life is full of mishaps.

Advice from a friend: "Just use the SWSW approach. So what if it goes well? So what if it doesn't?"

In either case, reflect. Make changes. And move forward.

In the beginning we spent a lot of time talking about problem-solving and how to react without overreacting. I taught drawing, which can be intimidating. Before they even started to draw, I would remind them, "What's the worst thing that can happen? You mess up and you have to start over? You know what starting over tells me? It tells me you give a crap."

In my first year of teaching, we spent the entire semester examining the life and work of more than a dozen famous artists. This material was over and above the course requirements of learning to draw. I had lofty notions. Everyone would be fully immersed in a rich art-history experience and swept away by my captivatingly dynamic PowerPoint presentations. I was definitely new to teaching.

By the end of the semester, we were prepared for a 120-slide college-survey-style exam that I administered to the entire class as a group. My administrators thought it was over the top, especially for my freshman students.

On exam day I had everyone building their standard standing manila-folder "houses" around their test space—completely cheat proof. We were all a nervous wreck, including me. This exam was 25 percent of their final grade. I collected study guides and flash cards, turned out the lights, and fired up the PowerPoint.

One of my thirty-five students raised their hand. "Uh . . . Mrs. Fox . . . you never gave us an answer sheet."

Yep. There they sat.

Pens in hand.

With no paper.

Rats.

I'd never printed the answer sheets.

As much as I talked a big game about taking it all in stride, I was fairly new at this teaching gig and suffering from impostor syndrome. Fearing the mockery or potential chaos from my lack of preparation (this is the stuff teachers' nightmares are made of), I was embarrassed to admit I had messed up.

The grace that followed my mishap almost made me cry.

One of my seniors spoke up. "What's the worst thing that can happen, Mrs. Fox? We wait five minutes so you can print the answer sheets? So what?"

Wow. A minor teacher trial met with adolescent grace and joy.

When we handle setbacks with joy, students see two things. First, they understand that trials will come. This verse says "when," not "if," we encounter various trials. Second, they experience the value of taking the trial in stride, with an approach that considers it joyfully instead of letting it take us to the mat. Teachable moments for handling pressure with grace are abundant in our classrooms. Education offers us a smorgasbord of trials every day.

God has given us a hopeful guideline here, that this kind of faith testing produces endurance. We educators need endurance—this profession is similar to running a marathon. Most trials are minimal, like my answer-sheet snafu. But some are gut-wrenching and riddled with hardship. It's in these times that our faith is truly tested. Knowing he is our fuel source, God's directive to consider trials as joy gives us the strength to maintain our pace until we cross the finish line. The joy is our part; the endurance is God's.

Remember our mantra: So what if it works? So what if it doesn't? It worked. We crushed that final exam with a 98 percent pass rate.

Rooted

See the trials for what they truly are: an opportunity to consider the joy and build the endurance of our faith.

Refreshed

Reflect on a trial in your classroom, great or small, when students witnessed you considering it all joy.

90
Not Who We Are

Rid yourself of a deceitful mouth
And keep devious speech far from you.

Proverbs 4:24

Teenage drama. Welcome to the secondary classroom.

Drama at this age is like a level-four whitewater-rafting adventure. Social media is the hurricane that upends the raft.

One day in class I overheard students discussing a new social media account featuring students from our school. Evidently students were snapping photos of kids in all sorts of embarrassing situations, from falling asleep in class to chewing their food at lunch, and even going so far as holding the phone over the bathroom stall to grab a shot. Yes, you read that right. It was a vile, humiliating display.

I had a personal policy to stay out of student drama, as it resolves itself quickly in most cases. I also had a strong suspicion that the owner of the account might be sitting in my classroom. This mess needed my attention, and fast.

Before I addressed the students, I touched base with admin to see if they were aware of the situation. They informed me that after some investigation, they were told the account had to be shut down by the owner. With no one coming forward, they were at a disciplinary standstill.

A teachable moment was in order. I decided to address the nastiness head on. I began with a simple statement. "This is *not* who we are."

You could hear a pin drop. They knew exactly what I was talking about.

"Tearing people down is bad enough, but tearing them down in front of the entire world is something else altogether. Each person in those images is someone's sister or brother, son or daughter. Someone's friend. Public humiliation is not acceptable. It's not what we do, and the owner of that page, whoever they are, needs to shut it down immediately."

I finished by casting my gaze over the room, intently staring into their eyes.

"You know who's doing this. I strongly suggest you speak to them about shutting it down."

Thirty-six sets of wide eyes stared back at me. Three girls were crying. The boys were silent. After class a young lady came up and thanked me. She said she had never had a teacher address a class this way. She said she felt like I really cared about the students in those pictures, and she knew some of them personally. They had been humiliated and traumatized by this experience.

In full Proverbs 4:24 fashion, devious speech was surely the origin of a stunt like this.

There is so much teen drama at the secondary education level that it is often tempting to look the other way, to ignore what we're hearing and focus on our own overextended agenda. It can also be tempting to do nothing but still vent and "spill the tea" to coworkers in the break room. The Enemy would love for us to wallow in the muck of deceitful speech and spread gossip like crop dust instead of taking a stand for what is right.

God always has a better plan. A plan that shares words of honesty, kindness, and courage to protect the students in our care. He gives a platform and the privilege to stand up in defense of the indefensible. In this case it was the unassuming people in those photos, humiliated on social media.

God's Word tells us to keep this kind of damaging speech—humiliating others—far from us. We serve a God who fights for the helpless and sets the example of kindness and compassion over a deceitful mouth. A conscience free of deceitful speech sends our students a message—they are safe in the shadow of our integrity.

To this day I have no idea who the owner of that account was, but by 3:00 p.m. it had vanished from social media.

Rooted

Protect your speech and guard your integrity so you can protect your students. They need you.

Refreshed

Reflect on a time when you chose to deflect deceitful speech and stand in the gap against injustice for your students.

When Never Meets Now

Dear Reader,

I'm hoping this last entry title isn't some kind of copyright violation—it'd be a heck of a thing to get this far and end up with a big fat C&D letter ("cease and desist," aka "don't rip off my title"), but I'm gonna take my chances, because this title is the only reason you're reading this.

"When Never Meets Now" is the title of a message preached by my pastor on January 16, 2022. I heard it three short months before we suddenly set the wheels in motion to relocate and be near our daughter and her husband.

God had been speaking to me about the move for months. Until that enlightening day in January, the Enemy had me convinced that I was incapable of leaving the classroom to pursue full-time art-curriculum design, much less write this book.

Thankfully, Satan is a liar. For almost two years I had cowered while he whispered the lies of my inability to do anything other than teach. He went so far as to tell me I would never be happy outside the classroom. Ever. Don't get me wrong—teaching was my dream job. I miss teaching terribly. Do I miss the bureaucracy? Uh . . . no.

During the message, my pastor said that one immediate action is worth a thousand words. He also said that God's past faithfulness is the best predictor of his future performance and that we won't know the truth about our calling until we obey the call. When we stop asking God to explain it and start trusting him, things change.

I was so busy focusing on the fear that I was drowning out the still, small voice of my Savior telling me to move forward into a new season, a new chapter, a new state: *I have an assignment for you, and it's way outside of your comfort zone. I have and will continue to equip you, but you must trust me.*

I also wrote these words in the margin of my message notes: "I am not chained to the limitations of the past. God is HERE for my new chapter. He is the Great I AM. He is here."

He's here for you too.

Whatever you're facing, or are about to face, God is with you. If you're still in the classroom, please remember that he has designed, appointed, and positioned each student to be in your care.

If you are new to this matchless profession, prepare for a life-changing career—your life and the lives of your blessed students. Call on him on the drive to school, in the middle of the chaos, and on the way home. He will meet you exactly where you are, and he will never leave you or forsake you.

If you are entering retirement, congratulations on a job well done. Thousands of children are better people because of your kindness and care. There is restful beauty in the days ahead.

As for me, I remain forever grateful for my thirteen fabulous years teaching high school. If you're reading this and you are one of my former students, I love you. My prayer for you is simple: Spend time with the One who made you, and center your life on his Word. This life will not be without its challenges, but God is ever present and always faithful in all circumstances, large and small. Trust him.

Thank you for spending ninety days with me as I returned to Lake Norman High School. God was in each moment, from my ten years in college to the thirteen years with my wonderful students.

I think I'll go sit with the Lord and do some more remembering... another ninety-day devotional awaits.

www.ingramcontent.com/pod-product-compliance
Ingram Content Group UK Ltd.
Pitfield, Milton Keynes, MK11 3LW, UK
UKHW021935200726
13853UKWH00011B/2146

9 798993 346700